THE UNOFFICIAL

ANIMAL CROSSING

COOKBOOK

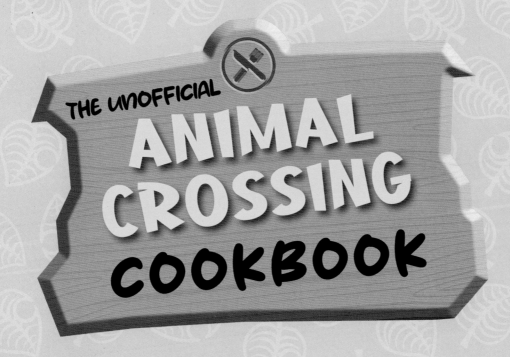

THE UNOFFICIAL ANIMAL CROSSING COOKBOOK

BY
TOM GRIMM

WITH PHOTOS BY
TOM GRIMM & DIMITRIE HARDER

REEL
INK
PRESS

CONTENTS

BAKED GOODS

DRINKS

LET'S GET COOKING!

Animal Crossing is one of the most popular video game franchises of all time. *New Horizons* alone, the latest game in the series, has sold more than 40 million copies, making it one of the most successful games ever. And instead of the dramatic explosions and deadly weapons found in many other video games, Animal Crossing serves up lovely graphics, cute characters, and a wealth of different tasks so players can keep growing and adding to their home on the island.

And just like in real life, food is an important part of life in Animal Crossing. As soon as you have a stove, a recipe, and the necessary ingredients, you can show off your culinary skill. On the islands of Animal Crossing, recipes can be acquired from neighbors and friends, and even in message bottles that wash up on the beach. In real life, you have this book, our message bottle to you. Inside, you'll find 60 recipes for appetizers, salads, soups, main dishes, side dishes, desserts, baked goods, and drinks from all over the world, all family-tested and easy to make, even for cooking novices! And every single dish is inspired by the world and characters of Animal Crossing. Some of them look like they came straight from the game! If you've ever wished you could reach into the screen and taste Franklin's Clam Chowder or Mom's Homemade Cake, this book is for you.

The Unofficial Animal Crossing Cookbook will tell you how to create the diverse cuisine of Animal Crossing right in your own kitchen. So what are you waiting for? Without further ado, let's get cooking!

STARTERS

Animal Crossing is full of memorable beginnings. Remember naming your island, or looking for a spot to put your tent, or even meeting Timmy and Tommy at the start of your island getaway? The recipes in this section will get any meal off to a great start and have everybody around the table eager for what comes next.

SALAD-STUFFED TOMATO

 15 MINUTES   **4 SERVINGS**   ★

Just like in real life, in Animal Crossing you can learn a lot of interesting things from your neighbors. Not just the latest gossip, but sometimes tasty recipes, too—like the one for these tomatoes featuring a hearty filling that will delight vegetarians and meat-eaters alike! Just visit another villager while they're cooking and ask what smells so good. If you're lucky, they'll tell you the recipe. So it pays to be nice!

1. Carefully cut the tomatoes crosswise about three-fourths of the way up. Remove the top piece like a lid. Use a spoon to carefully hollow out the tomatoes to a depth of about 2 inches, being sure to keep the outer part intact.

2. Preheat the oven to 300°F. Line a baking sheet with parchment paper.

3. Place the avocado and lime juice in a medium bowl. Add the mozzarella, bell pepper, sun-dried tomatoes, scallions, oil, and basil. Stir well to combine and season to taste with salt and black pepper.

4. Transfer the filling to the hollowed-out tomatoes, mounding the filling slightly, then sprinkle with cheese. Place the tomatoes a couple of inches apart on the prepared baking sheet and bake for 5 to 7 minutes, until the cheese is melted. Remove, allow them to cool briefly, and garnish each one with a basil leaf to serve.

INGREDIENTS

*4 large beefsteak tomatoes
(each about 10 ounces)*

2 avocados, pitted, peeled, and diced

Juice of 1 lime

Two 4.5-ounce balls mozzarella, diced

1 yellow bell pepper, diced

3 sun-dried tomatoes, minced

*½ bunch scallions, white and green parts,
thinly sliced into rings*

1 tablespoon canola oil

*¼ bunch fresh basil, finely chopped,
plus whole leaves for garnish*

Salt

Ground black pepper

Shredded cheese for topping

OLIVIER SALAD

 30 MINUTES, PLUS 1 HOUR TO CHILL   4 SERVINGS   ★

Olivier Salad is a traditional salad dish served at holidays in Russian cuisine, and it's also popular in other post-Soviet countries. Typically served to celebrate the New Year, the dish is named for its creator, Lucien Olivier (1838–1883), who operated the famed Hermitage French restaurant in Moscow in 1864. The recipe for the sauce used in this hearty, creamy classic was a particularly closely guarded secret. Olivier is said to have taken it with him to the grave—but that can't be true, since his recipe was obviously passed down *somehow*. Otherwise, it wouldn't be possible to get Olivier salad in Animal Crossing on January 1, and only then, to mark the New Year . . . would it?

1. Combine the potatoes and carrots in a large pot of water and bring to a boil over high heat. Reduce the heat to maintain a simmer for 15 to 20 minutes, or until the vegetables are tender. Drain the vegetables in a colander.

2. Meanwhile, place the sausage, onion, pickles, pickle juice, peas, eggs, apple, and mayonnaise in a large bowl and stir a few times to combine. Add the cooked vegetables to the bowl. Stir well to combine and season generously with salt and black pepper. Stir in the minced dill.

3. Cover the bowl loosely with plastic wrap and refrigerate for at least 1 hour to meld the flavors. Before serving, stir thoroughly to combine. Pour off any excess liquid and garnish with parsley.

INGREDIENTS

10.5 ounces potatoes, diced

5 ounces carrots, peeled and diced

15 ounces dense, smooth cooked sausage such as bologna, diced

5 ounces onion, diced

3.5 ounces pickles, diced

½ cup pickle juice

10 ounces canned peas, drained

3 hard-boiled eggs, diced

1 tart apple, diced

5 ounces mayonnaise

Salt

Ground black pepper

½ bunch fresh dill, minced

Chopped fresh parsley for garnish

TIP OF THE DAY

Like most potato salads, this one tastes even better if left to rest so the flavors meld. It is best refrigerated overnight, covered with plastic wrap. If you do this, let the salad return to room temperature before serving.

NANAKUSA GAYU

 25 MINUTES   2 TO 3 SERVINGS   ⟨★⟩ ★

This rice porridge is traditionally served during the Japanese festival of *Nanakusa-no-sekku*, the "Festival of Seven Herbs," on January 7. According to a time-honored tradition, a bowl of the porridge is placed on a wooden cutting board that day, along with a rice scoop, and then a special declaration is made: "Before the birds from the continent fly to Japan, let's eat *nanakusa!*" Things are a little less formal in Animal Crossing, but even there, nanakusa gayu is only offered as part of the relevant seasonal events—which is quite a shame, actually, since this rice porridge is simply delectable, in spite of its humble look! Good thing you can now enjoy it whenever you like, thanks to this recipe.

1. In a medium saucepan over medium heat, combine the rice, chicken broth, and salt. Bring to a boil, then immediately lower the heat to low, cover, and simmer until about half the liquid has been absorbed, about 15 minutes. Add the radish and simmer, covered, for another 10 minutes, stirring frequently so the dish does not burn and stick to the pan.

2. Remove the rice from the heat and add the butter to melt. Fold in the cilantro and season with the powdered bouillon and sesame oil. Combine thoroughly so the rice is nice and creamy throughout.

3. Stir in the scallion and serve sprinkled with white and black sesame seed.

INGREDIENTS

1¼ cups rice

2⅔ cups chicken broth

1 teaspoon salt

3.5 ounces daikon radish, peeled and diced

2 tablespoons butter

2 tablespoons minced fresh cilantro or watercress

1 teaspoon, or 1 cube, powdered bouillon

1 teaspoon sesame oil

1 scallion, green part only, thinly cut into rings

Pinch white sesame seed

Pinch black sesame seed

OMURICE

This traditional Japanese omelet is known by various names, including omurice and omuraisu. Originating in the early 20th century, it's a popular dish in Japan and beyond, including your island, where you can get the recipe at Nook's Cranny (for a whopping 1,400 Bells). This hearty dish of eggs, rice, chicken, and aromatic tomato sauce may seem complicated. But don't worry! It's so easy to make that even a lazybones like Leonardo could manage it.

1. In a medium skillet over medium heat, warm the oil until it shimmers. Add the onion and sweat until translucent, about 2 to 3 minutes. Add the chicken and lightly brown on all sides, about 6 to 8 minutes. Add the diced tomatoes, bell pepper, mushrooms, and powdered bouillon, stirring well to combine. Season to taste with salt and black pepper. Cook for 2 minutes, then stir in the cooked rice and heat through.

2. Meanwhile, prepare one omelet per person. Melt a bit of butter in a large skillet over medium heat. Combine the eggs and heavy cream in a medium bowl and season generously with salt and black pepper. Once the butter is hot, pour a third of the mixture evenly into the pan so the entire base of the pan is covered, then cook (without stirring) until set and the top is firm, 3 to 4 minutes. Carefully flip the omelet with a pancake turner and cook on the other side for 2 to 3 minutes, until set. Place the omelet onto a large plate. Repeat this process with the remaining egg mixture.

3. Top the front half of each omelet with as much chicken filling as desired and then fold the back half of the omelet over the filling. Sprinkle with parsley and serve garnished with a dollop of tomato sauce.

INGREDIENTS

1 tablespoon neutral oil

1 onion, diced

5 ounces boneless, skinless chicken breast, diced

3.5 ounces canned diced tomatoes

1 green bell pepper, diced

6 mushrooms, diced

1 teaspoon, or 1 cube, powdered bouillon

Salt

Ground black pepper

1 cup cooked rice
(preferably from the day before)

Butter for the pan

6 eggs

⅔ cup heavy cream

Minced fresh parsley for garnish

Tomato sauce (page 34)

SOUPS

In the busy world of Animal Crossing, the soup selection is small but varied, reflecting different seasons and cultures that are part of the AC mix. Hopefully you'll find one of your favorites on this short list and be inspired to try something new as well.

BAMBOO-SHOOT SOUP

🕐 50 MINUTES (INCL. SOAKING TIME)   🍲 4 SERVINGS   ★

Edible shoots of various species of bamboo are used in many Asian dishes, including this hearty traditional soup. It's a perfect pick-me-up after a hard day's work in the garden. On your island, you have to buy a whole bunch of turnips from Daisy Mae before she'll send you the recipe in the mail. It's a little strange, since there aren't any turnips in this soup!

1. Place the mushrooms in a small bowl. Pour boiling water over them and soak for 30 minutes. Carefully drain the mushrooms, squeeze them to remove the excess liquid, and cut them into strips.

2. Place the chicken stock in a medium saucepan. Add the mushrooms, pork, and bamboo shoots. Bring to a boil over medium heat, then lower the heat and simmer for 10 minutes.

3. In a small dish, stir together the cornstarch and cold water until smooth, then stir the slurry into the soup. Add the soy sauce, rice wine vinegar, and sesame oil. Season to taste with salt and white pepper. Add the tofu and simmer for 3 minutes.

4. Stir the beaten egg into the soup. Briefly allow the egg to set, then divide the soup among serving bowls. Serve sprinkled with the scallions.

INGREDIENTS

0.35 ounces dried wood ear (mu-err) mushrooms

3⅓ cups chicken stock

7 ounces pork neck, cut into bite-size pieces

10 ounces canned sliced bamboo shoots, drained

2 tablespoons cornstarch

1 to 2 tablespoons cold water

3 tablespoons soy sauce

1 tablespoon rice wine vinegar

2 tablespoons sesame oil

Salt

Ground white pepper

4 ounces tofu, diced

1 egg, beaten

2 scallions, green part only, thinly cut into rings

CLAM CHOWDER

 30 MINUTES   4 SERVINGS   ★ ★

Legend has it that the basic recipe for this traditional seafood soup originated in France and was brought to New England in the 17th or 18th century by French seafarers, who were forced to adjust the recipe to reflect the ingredients available locally. The modified version of this hearty and elegant dish spread from there to become a culinary sensation all over the world. The dish even made it to your Animal Crossing island, where Franklin cooks this chowder for Turkey Day every year. He gives his famed recipe to anyone who brings him a few Manila clams and scallops.

1. In a large Dutch oven over medium heat, melt the butter. Add the onion and garlic and sweat until translucent but not brown, about 2 to 3 minutes. Stir in the bacon and sauté briefly on all sides. Sprinkle with the flour and sauté, stirring constantly, for 5 minutes. Add the stock, potatoes, and celery, stirring well to combine. Maintain a simmer (adjusting the heat as necessary) for 10 minutes, or until the vegetables are cooked but not too tender.

2. Meanwhile, scrub the mussels clean with a brush and discard the ones that have already opened. Add the clean mussels and scallops to the soup and simmer for 10 minutes. Remove and discard all the mussels that have not opened (these are not safe to eat).

3. Stir in the milk, heavy cream, and wine and season to taste with lemon juice, salt, and black pepper. Finally, add the dill, stir again to combine, and serve.

INGREDIENTS

1 tablespoon butter

1 onion, diced

1 garlic clove, minced

2.6 ounces bacon, diced

1 tablespoon all-purpose flour

2½ cups fish or chicken stock

9 ounces russet potatoes, diced

3.5 ounces celery, thinly sliced

18 ounces fresh mussels

7 ounces frozen scallops, thawed

½ cup plus 2 teaspoons whole milk

½ cup plus 2 teaspoons heavy cream

⅔ cup dry white wine

Squeeze lemon juice

Salt

Ground black pepper

½ bunch fresh dill, minced

TIP OF THE DAY

It's okay to omit the wine from this recipe. You may need to add a bit more lemon juice when seasoning.

MINESTRONE SOUP

 1 HOUR & 30 MINUTES   6 SERVINGS   ★ ★

Minestrone is one of the main classics of Italian cuisine, which isn't exactly short on classics. The ancient Romans were already making a type of vegetable soup containing pretty much everything found in their local gardens and forests some 2,000 years ago. More ingredients were added over time as the Romans brought them home from their military campaigns. You don't have to invade any foreign countries to make *this* recipe, though—all it takes is a trip to the supermarket, at least in the real world. In the world of Animal Crossing, it's worthwhile to stop by your neighbors' place when they're making something to eat. With luck, they just might give you the recipe for this delicious soup!

1. In a large pot over medium heat, melt the butter and warm the oil until it shimmers. Add the pancetta and cook for 2 minutes, until brown on all sides. Add the onion and garlic and sweat until translucent. Add the potatoes, carrot, and celery and stir well to combine. Sauté for 2 minutes, then stir in the beans and zucchini. Sauté for another 2 minutes. Then cover and cook the vegetables, stirring occasionally, for 15 minutes, until the vegetables are cooked.

2. Add the stock, diced tomatoes, tomato paste, basil, and Parmesan. Season to taste with salt and black pepper. Add the oregano to taste. Bring to a brief boil, then lower the heat to low and simmer gently, stirring occasionally, for 1 hour.

3. To serve, sprinkle with additional grated Parmesan.

INGREDIENTS

4 tablespoons butter

¼ cup olive oil

2 ounces pancetta, diced

3 large onions, diced

3 garlic cloves, minced

3 large potatoes, diced

1 carrot, diced

½ rib celery, thinly sliced

5 ounces canned white beans, drained

1 zucchini, thinly sliced

6¼ cups vegetable or chicken stock

3.5 ounces canned diced tomatoes

2 tablespoons tomato paste

1 bunch fresh basil, minced

3.5 ounces grated Parmesan cheese, plus more for garnish

Salt

Ground black pepper

Pinch dried oregano, or more as needed

PUMPKIN SOUP

CONTAINS ALCOHOL

 1 HOUR   4 SERVINGS   ⭐ ★ ★

Fall is pumpkin season in Animal Crossing (and in real life). All through October, you can buy pumpkin seeds from various sources, including Timmy and Tommy at Nook's Cranny. You can plant the seeds and then use the pumpkins to make a whole range of spooky Halloween items or to cook this tasty soup! Lucky players will find the recipe in a message in a bottle on the beach. Alternatively, feel free to use *this* recipe and save yourself the bother of looking! You do still have to get the pumpkin on your own, though. Jack, the Czar of Halloween, might be able to help you with that. Or visit your local farmer's market!

1. Preheat the oven to 175°F. Line a baking sheet with parchment paper.

2. With a tablespoon, carefully scrape out all seeds and strings from the pumpkin and discard. Leaving the rind on, coarsely chop the pumpkin into pieces. Place on the prepared baking sheet and bake for 20 minutes. Remove the baking sheet from the oven and pour off any excess liquid.

3. Heat the butter in a large pot over medium heat until it melts. Add the shallot and garlic and cook until the garlic is translucent, about 2 to 3 minutes. Add the pumpkin, stir to combine, and sauté briefly. Add the potatoes, carrots, and broccoli. Sprinkle the flour and paprika over the top and stir well to combine. Add the broth, wine, and coconut milk. Bring to a brief boil, then lower the heat to low, cover, and simmer for about 25 minutes, stirring occasionally. Remove from the heat.

4. Add the ginger and curry powder. Use an immersion blender to purée the soup in the pot, then add the heavy cream and season generously with salt and black pepper to taste. Garnish with pumpkin seeds and a bit of parsley to serve.

INGREDIENTS

One 3-pound blue Hokkaido pumpkin (blue kuri squash), quartered

2 tablespoons butter

2 shallots, minced

1 garlic clove, minced

9 ounces potatoes, diced

2 carrots, finely grated

1 head broccoli, florets only

2 tablespoons all-purpose flour

1 teaspoon paprika

3⅓ cups vegetable broth

¾ cup plus 2 tablespoons white wine

3.5 ounces canned coconut milk

One 1-inch piece fresh ginger, finely grated

3 tablespoons curry powder

¼ cup heavy cream

Salt

Ground black pepper

Toasted or roasted pumpkin seeds (pepitas) for garnish

Chopped fresh parsley for garnish

TIP OF THE DAY

If you'd like to omit the wine from this recipe, add a splash of vinegar instead to give the soup a bit of acidity. And if you want to serve your soup exactly as shown in the game, you'll need a second pumpkin, which should be hollowed out as described in step 1 and used as a serving bowl.

SEAWEED SOUP

 2 HOURS & 30 MINUTES 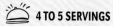 4 TO 5 SERVINGS ★ ★

This seaweed soup is a time-honored dish originating in Korean cuisine. In most areas of the country, it's traditionally served to mark birthdays and other special occasions. In some regions the soup is an everyday staple, since the ocean is right next door, with all its bounty. Just like on your island, where a seaweed soup recipe is included with the basic recipe set at Nook's Cranny.

1. Rinse the shank, rib steak, and marrow bones thoroughly. Transfer them to a large Dutch oven or pot. Add the vegetables, then pour in the vegetable broth, beef stock, and fish broth. If the meat is not completely covered with liquid, add water to cover. Bring to a boil over medium heat, then adjust the heat to maintain a simmer for 30 minutes, regularly skimming off the foam that forms on the top. Then lower the heat to low and simmer gently for 2 hours.

2. Meanwhile, soak the seaweed in a large bowl of cold water for 30 minutes, or until it has expanded considerably. Then remove the seaweed from the bowl, squeeze out all excess moisture, and use a large, sharp knife to cut it into bite-size pieces.

3. In a medium skillet over medium heat, warm the oil until it shimmers. Add the chicken and cook on all sides for 6 to 8 minutes, or until the meat is just cooked through and light golden brown. Season lightly with salt.

4. Strain the broth through a fine-mesh strainer into a large clean pot. Discard the vegetables and marrow bones. Allow the meat on the shank and rib steak to cool a bit, then remove the meat from the bone and shred it into small pieces. Add the meat, garlic, and seaweed to the broth and simmer for 2 to 3 minutes over medium heat. Season to taste with soy sauce.

5. Divide the seaweed soup among the serving bowls and garnish each with cooked chicken. Sprinkle with toasted sesame and serve immediately.

INGREDIENTS

One 10-ounce beef shank crosscut

One 7-ounce flat rib steak

2 to 3 marrow bones

1 bunch soup vegetables, diced

2 cups vegetable broth

2 cups beef stock

2 cups fish broth

3.5 ounces dried brown seaweed

1 tablespoon neutral oil

9 ounces chicken breast fillet, cut into bite-size pieces

Salt

2 garlic cloves, minced

Soy sauce

Toasted white sesame seed

MAINS

The food choices in Animal Crossing include iconic dishes from all over the globe, and that's particularly true for this batch of recipes. In the spirit of Nook Inc., consider this to be your ticket for a culinary getaway, with stops in Hawaii, Japan, Italy, Thailand, and points beyond.

NEW YEAR'S NOODLES

 25 MINUTES 2 TO 3 SERVINGS ⭐

In Japan, the New Year is traditionally welcomed with *toshikoshi soba,* a noodle dish said to enhance good fortune over the next 12 months by symbolically "cutting ties" with the past, because the soba noodles in this dish are very soft and effortless to cut. Right in line with the old Japanese custom, New Year's Noodles can only be obtained at Nook's Cranny during the Ōmisoka event, which runs from December 25 to 31. That's too bad, because this rich soup is much too tasty to serve only one week out of the year. Believe me, once you've tasted them, you'll want to enjoy New Year's Noodles as often as possible!

1. Cook the soba noodles according to the package instructions in a large pot of generously salted water until done, usually about 6 to 8 minutes. Drain well and run under cold water to cool.

2. Meanwhile, bring the dashi to a simmer in a medium saucepan over medium heat. Stir in the soy sauce and mirin, add the beef, and simmer for 10 to 12 minutes, or until the meat is done but still juicy.

3. Divide the cooked noodles among serving bowls, pour the broth over them, and add some of the meat to each serving. Garnish with a few slices of narutomaki and sprinkle with scallions.

4. Serve immediately.

INGREDIENTS

7 ounces soba noodles

Salt

2 cups dashi or beef broth

3 tablespoons plus 1 teaspoon soy sauce

2 tablespoons mirin

9 ounces beef, cut into bite-size pieces

½ store-bought roll narutomaki, cut into ¾-inch slices

1 scallion, green part only, thinly sliced into rings

GNOCCHI DI CAROTE

CONTAINS ALCOHOL

 2 HOURS & 10 MINUTES 4 SERVINGS ★ ★ ★

On your island, you can whip up a delectable serving of gnocchi di carote with just flour and carrots. In real life, you do need more ingredients to make this hearty vegetarian dish. But you can easily find them all on a quick trip to your local supermarket. Plus, since you have this cookbook, you don't have to spend hours combing the beach hoping to find the recipe inside a bottle. You can get started once you've gathered all the ingredients. Buon appetito!

To make the tomato sauce:

1. In a medium saucepan over medium heat, warm the oil until it shimmers. Add the onion and garlic and sweat until translucent, about 2 to 3 minutes. Add the diced tomatoes, tomato paste, and sun-dried tomatoes. Stir to combine and sauté for a few minutes, then deglaze the pan with the red wine. Stir in the thyme, rosemary, salt, black pepper, and sugar. Lower the heat to low and simmer, uncovered, for 1 hour, stirring frequently. Add the parsley and oregano and reduce for 1 hour more. If too much liquid evaporates in the process, add water.

2. Remove and discard the rosemary sprig. Season to taste with added salt, black pepper, and sugar.

To make the carrot gnocchi:

3. Place the potatoes in a large pot of generously salted water over medium heat. Bring to a boil, then cook for about 20 minutes, or until soft. Drain and allow them to stand so the steam evaporates.

4. Meanwhile, in a medium skillet over medium heat, warm the oil until it shimmers. Add the carrots, water, and 1 tablespoon of salt and cook for 15 minutes, until the carrots are tender. Allow the carrots to cool briefly, then put them in a food processor and purée until smooth.

5. Press the potatoes through a potato ricer into a large bowl. Add the carrot purée, egg yolks, flour, pinch of black pepper, and a bit of salt. Use your hands to knead everything together until a dough forms.

INGREDIENTS

For the Tomato Sauce
1 tablespoon olive oil

1 onion, diced

2 garlic cloves, minced

One 14-ounce can diced tomatoes

1 tablespoon tomato paste

0.5 ounces sun-dried tomatoes, minced

3 tablespoons plus 1 teaspoon red wine

1 teaspoon dried thyme

1 sprig fresh rosemary

1 tablespoon salt

1 teaspoon ground black pepper

1½ teaspoons turbinado or raw sugar

¼ bunch fresh parsley, minced

¼ bunch fresh oregano, minced

TIP OF THE DAY
If you like, the red wine can be omitted from the tomato sauce.

6. Lightly flour a surface. Transfer the dough to the surface and shape into a long rope about 1¼ inches in diameter. Use a large, sharp knife to cut into ¾-inch-thick pieces. Shape the pieces into balls and gently press flat with a fork on both sides.

7. Transfer the shaped gnocchi to a large pot of generously salted boiling water. Cook for 2 to 3 minutes, or until they rise to the surface on their own. Then remove the gnocchi and drain.

8. In a medium skillet over medium heat, melt the butter. Add the drained gnocchi and sauté on all sides for 1 to 2 minutes. Season with salt and black pepper.

9. Arrange the gnocchi in bowls or deep plates, top with tomato sauce, and serve garnished with fresh basil.

For the Carrot Gnocchi

2 pounds russet potatoes, peeled

Salt

1 tablespoon olive oil

4 large carrots, peeled and sliced thinly across

¼ cup water

2 egg yolks

¾ cup plus 4 teaspoons all-purpose flour, plus more for the counter

Ground black pepper

4 tablespoons butter

Fresh basil for garnish

Also required:
Potato ricer

PAD KRAPOW

⏱ 25 MINUTES   🍲 4 SERVINGS   💰 ★ ★

Practically the unofficial national dish of Thailand, pad krapow is available on almost any street corner there. The name means "stir-fried holy basil," a nod to the most exotic ingredient in this dish: Thai basil. You won't find any Thai basil, which has a slightly peppery flavor, in Animal Crossing, though the recipe for pad krapow can be purchased at Nook's Cranny. In the real world, try your luck at an Asian grocery store. You can also make this dish using cloves and allspice. Just don't tell Franklin! He gets really worked up about things like that.

1. Combine the garlic, shallots, and chile in a mortar and use the pestle to crush the ingredients into a fine smooth paste.

2. Place the oil (yes, all of it!) in a wok or heavy-bottomed skillet and warm over medium heat until it shimmers. Add one egg and cook until the bottom side is firm, about 4 to 6 minutes, then carefully use a pancake turner to loosen the edges of the egg from the wok. Hold the wok at an angle and use a spoon to scoop hot oil over the parts where the white of the egg is still transparent. Once the egg has reached the desired consistency, use the pancake turner to carefully transfer it to a large plate. Cover with aluminum foil to keep warm. Repeat this process with the remaining three eggs.

3. Pour off the excess oil from the wok, leaving 1 tablespoon. Heat over medium heat, then add the chile paste. Cook, stirring constantly, until fragrant, about 2 to 3 minutes. Then add the pork and cook until brown on all sides but not bone-dry, 5 to 6 minutes.

4. Add the fish sauce, light and dark soy sauces, oyster sauce, and coconut sugar and stir well to combine. Add the Thai basil leaves and briefly cook until the basil starts to wilt, but do not brown.

5. Divide the cooked rice among serving bowls, top with meat and sauce, and place a fried egg on top of each serving. Garnish with a bit of basil and serve immediately.

INGREDIENTS

2 garlic cloves, minced

2 shallots, minced

*1 red bird's eye chile (Thai chile),
finely chopped*

½ cup neutral oil

4 eggs

14 ounces pork, cut into bite-size pieces

2 tablespoons fish sauce

1 tablespoon light soy sauce

1 tablespoon dark soy sauce

1 tablespoon oyster sauce

1 tablespoon coconut sugar

*1 bunch fresh Thai basil, stemmed,
plus more for garnish*

*4 servings rice, preferably jasmine rice
(see page 39)*

Also required:
Mortar and pestle

Wok (or medium heavy-bottomed skillet)

CURRY WITH RICE

⏱ **45 MINUTES** 🍽 **4 SERVINGS** 💰 ★ ★

Curry is among the world's most popular dishes. And no wonder; it is extraordinarily versatile. With just a few ingredients, it can be adapted to practically any taste and dietary preference, whether made with fish or meat or in a vegetarian or vegan style. And since the Animal Crossing islands are known for being home to as much variety as possible, this curry dish with rice is a Café menu mainstay. Eat it for five energy points. In the real world, too, this hearty dish will give you enough energy to put all your big plans into motion!

1. Combine the rice and water in a medium saucepan. Add the salt and allow the rice to soften for 10 minutes.

2. Bring the rice to a boil over medium heat, then cover, reduce the heat to low, and simmer until the water has evaporated completely, about 15 minutes. Do not stir during this stage.

3. Remove the rice from the heat and add the butter to melt. Combine thoroughly so the butter is nicely distributed throughout the rice.

4. While the rice is cooking, prepare the curry. In a large skillet over medium heat, warm the oil until it shimmers. Add the onions, garlic, and ginger and sauté, stirring, for several minutes, until the vegetables are soft. Stir in the tomato paste, garam masala, and curry powder and cook for 30 seconds. Stir in the diced tomatoes and coconut milk. Add the chicken pieces, stir well to combine, and cook, stirring occasionally, for 15 minutes, or until the chicken is cooked through. Season to taste. Stir in the chile.

5. Arrange the cooked rice on one side of the plate with the curry on the other side. Garnish the rice with pickled red ginger and serve immediately.

INGREDIENTS

2 cups basmati or jasmine rice

3 cups water

1 teaspoon salt

2 tablespoons butter

2 tablespoons canola oil

2 onions, diced

2 garlic cloves, minced

One 1-inch piece fresh ginger, finely grated

1 tablespoon tomato paste

2 tablespoons garam masala

2 tablespoons curry powder

7 ounces canned diced tomatoes

One 13.5-ounce can coconut milk

18 ounces boneless, skinless chicken breast, cut into bite-size pieces

1 small green chile, thinly cut into rings

Jarred pickled red ginger, drained, for garnish

FISH AND CHIPS

🕐 1 HOUR 🍽 4 SERVINGS 💰⭐ ★ ★

A fish and chips dinner is as beloved in Britain as pasta in Italy, paella in Spain, or Peking duck in China. An absolute winner, this dish is also hugely popular among Animal Crossing residents. All you need to prepare it in the game is 2x potato and 1x dab. You'll need a few more ingredients to make this recipe in real life, but eating it will give you much more than five energy points—you'll also be left feeling pleasantly full and content!

To make the fried fish:

1. If necessary, use tweezers to remove the bones from the fish fillets. Sprinkle them with the lemon juice and season generously on both sides with salt and black pepper.

2. Spread the flour evenly on a plate. Place the eggs on a second plate or in a shallow bowl and whisk with a fork until the whites and yolks are combined. Pour the bread crumbs on a third plate.

3. Press one side of the fish into the flour, then the other side. Shake to remove excess flour. Then dredge the fish through the eggs so it is covered on all sides, and finally dredge in the bread crumbs.

4. In one or two large skillets over medium heat, melt the clarified butter. Carefully place the fillets in the skillet(s) and fry for 4 minutes on one side. Carefully turn and fry for another 4 minutes on the second side.

To make the potato wedges:

5. Preheat the oven to 350°F. Line a baking sheet with parchment paper.

6. Leaving the peel on, quarter the potatoes. In a large bowl, combine the oil, garlic, salt, black pepper, and paprika. Add the potatoes and toss until well coated. Transfer the potatoes to the prepared baking sheet. Bake for 40 to 50 minutes, turning occasionally, until crisp and golden brown.

To make the lemon sour cream:

7. In a small bowl, stir together the sour cream, chives, and lemon juice. Season generously with salt and black pepper. Cover with plastic wrap and refrigerate until used. Stir to combine again before using.

To assemble:

8. Place one fillet on each of four serving plates, garnish with a lemon wedge, and serve with the potato wedges, a bit of lemon sour cream, and ketchup.

INGREDIENTS

Four 6-ounce fish fillets, such as redfish, pollock, pangasius, or tilapia

2 tablespoons lemon juice

Salt

Ground black pepper

¼ cup all-purpose flour

2 eggs

¾ cup bread crumbs

3 tablespoons clarified butter (ghee)

For the Potato Wedges
2 pounds firm, waxy potatoes, scrubbed and dried well

¼ cup neutral oil

2 garlic cloves, pressed

1½ teaspoons salt

1½ teaspoons ground black pepper

1½ teaspoons paprika

For the Lemon Sour Cream
⅔ cup sour cream

2 tablespoons minced fresh chives

1 tablespoon lemon juice

Salt

Ground black pepper

For Assembly
4 lemon wedges

Ketchup for serving

PIZZA MARGHERITA

 40 MINUTES, PLUS 2½ HOURS TO RISE   4 SERVINGS   ★ ★

For decades now, pizza has consistently emerged the winner in every survey asking about the world's most popular dish. In 1889, King Umberto I and Queen Margherita di Savoia were visiting Naples, the birthplace of pizza, and famed pizzaiolo Raffaele Esposito made them a pizza topped with mozzarella, basil, and tomatoes in honor of the colors of the Italian flag. The queen was so thrilled that Esposito named it "Pizza Margherita" in the queen's honor. Then, when millions of Italians emigrated toward the end of the 19th century, pizza Margherita went along and became a hit all over the world. That's quite a success story!

To make the pizza dough:

1. Whisk together the flour, salt, and yeast in a large bowl. Add the water. Use a rubber spatula to mix until a sticky dough forms. Cover with plastic wrap and allow it to rise at room temperature for about 90 minutes, until doubled in size.

2. Generously flour a work surface. Turn out the dough on the work surface and divide into four pieces. Flour your hands and roll each piece into a ball. (The dough is sticky. Use as much flour as you need to make it manageable.) Do not overknead. Set the dough balls on a lightly floured baking sheet, about 4 inches apart. Sprinkle with flour, cover with a clean dish cloth, and allow them to rise at room temperature for another hour.

3. At the end of the rising time, preheat the oven to 475°F. Set a baking sheet in the bottom third of the oven.

To make the tomato sauce:

4. While the dough rises, in a medium saucepan over medium heat, warm the oil until it shimmers. Add the onions and sweat for 5 minutes, until translucent. Add the sugar and a small pinch of salt. Add the tomato paste and cook all the ingredients together briefly. Add the tomato purée and water and stir well to combine.

5. Add the bay leaves, basil, and marjoram. Bring to a boil, then lower the heat to low. Simmer for 10 to 15 minutes, stirring frequently, to meld the flavors.

INGREDIENTS

For the Pizza Dough
4 cups plus 8 teaspoons all-purpose flour, plus a bit more
1 teaspoon salt
⅓ of a 0.6-ounce cube (cake) fresh yeast
2 teaspoons kosher salt
1 teaspoon instant yeast
1¾ to 2 cups water, lukewarm

For the Tomato Sauce
3 tablespoons olive oil
2 onions, diced
1 teaspoon sugar, plus more as needed
Salt
1 tablespoon tomato paste
17 ounces canned tomato purée
⅔ cup water
2 bay leaves
8 fresh basil leaves
1 teaspoon dried marjoram
2 tablespoons butter
Ground black pepper

6. Remove and discard the bay leaves. Use an immersion blender to purée the sauce. Add the butter and purée again. Season with salt and black pepper to taste. Add a bit more sugar as needed.

To assemble:
7. Roll out one of the balls of dough on a floured surface, working from the inside out, until you have a round crust that is as thin as possible (about 9½ inches in diameter). Spread a quarter of the tomato sauce in an even layer over the crust. Top as desired with tomato slices, olives, and mozzarella and set on a sheet of parchment paper. Use the parchment paper to help transfer the pizza to the hot baking sheet, then bake in the bottom third of the oven for 10 to 12 minutes, or until the crust is as crispy as you like it.

8. Remove the pizza from the oven and garnish with freshly torn basil leaves before serving. Follow the same steps with the remaining dough and other ingredients. Enjoy right away.

For Assembly
4 tomatoes, sliced

One 4-ounce can black olives, drained and thinly sliced

Two 4.5-ounce balls fresh mozzarella di bufala, finely torn

1 bunch fresh basil, stemmed

BREAD GRATIN

 40 MINUTES   4 SERVINGS   ★ ★

Bread gratin is traditionally exactly what the name suggests: a type of gratin that—spoiler alert—is made mainly from bread. You can get the recipe for this bread gratin at various places around your island, including from the cook at the restaurant in *Happy Home Paradise*, where all you need to prepare this dish is 2x flour and 2x whole-wheat flour. Admittedly, that doesn't exactly sound like it's bursting with flavor. That's why the real-world ingredient list is a bit longer.

1. Preheat the oven to 350°F. Line a baking sheet with parchment paper.

2. Heat the oil in a medium pot over high heat. Add the onions and sweat until translucent, about 2 to 3 minutes. Add the carrots, bell peppers, and mushrooms, stir well to combine, and sauté for 4 minutes, stirring occasionally, until the vegetables are soft. Season with the salt, black pepper, and marjoram. Remove from the heat.

3. Use a bread knife to carefully cut off the top one-fifth of the bread. Hollow out the bread with your fingers, making sure the walls remain undamaged and thick enough to hold the gratin. Set the "bread lid" aside.

4. Combine the eggs, wine, heavy cream, parsley, and cheese in a large bowl. Add the cooked vegetables and stir well to combine. Transfer the mixture to the hollowed-out loaf of bread, set it on the prepared baking sheet, and sprinkle with more cheese. Bake for approximately 15 to 20 minutes. Then top with the "lid" and bake for another 5 minutes.

5. Remove the gratin from the oven and allow it to cool for several minutes. Serve promptly.

INGREDIENTS

2 tablespoons neutral oil

2 onions, diced

2 carrots, peeled and diced

½ red bell pepper, diced

½ yellow bell pepper, diced

½ green bell pepper, diced

7 ounces mushrooms, thinly sliced

Pinch salt

Pinch ground black pepper

Pinch dried marjoram

1 round loaf crusty bread

4 eggs

Scant ½ cup dry white wine

¾ cup plus 2 tablespoons heavy cream

Minced fresh parsley for garnish

7 ounces shredded cheese, such as Swiss, plus more for sprinkling

TIP OF THE DAY

Feel free to omit the white wine from this recipe. You can also cube the hollowed-out part of the bread and fry the pieces with some butter in a skillet for about 4 minutes to make golden-brown croutons. Then add a bit of salt and serve with all kinds of soup or a green salad.

SPAGHETTI CARBONARA

 25 MINUTES   4 SERVINGS   ★ ★

Surveys show that pasta is the most popular food in the world after pizza. The Chinese were the first to come up with the idea of making dough out of flour and water and boiling the dough instead of baking it. But it was the Italians who made pasta what it is today, serving it not just as an addition to soup, but with sauce as a main course. There are a dozen different pasta recipes to discover on your island in Animal Crossing, including this one for classic spaghetti carbonara.

1. In a large pot of generously salted water, cook the spaghetti according to the package instructions until it is al dente, usually about 6 minutes. Reserve ½ cup of pasta water, then drain.

2. Meanwhile, whisk the eggs in a medium bowl and stir in the Parmesan. Season generously with black pepper and a small pinch of salt.

3. In a very large skillet over medium heat, warm the oil until it shimmers. Add the pancetta and sauté on all sides until crisp, about 4 to 5 minutes. Turn off the heat, add the garlic, and cook in the remaining heat until fragrant. Then remove from the heat and allow the mixture to cool slightly—this is important to make sure the egg mixture does not clump together right away.

4. Add the drained spaghetti to the skillet and stir well to combine with the pancetta and pan drippings. Add the heavy cream and egg mixture and stir well again to combine. Add the reserved pasta water by tablespoons until the sauce has taken on the desired consistency and the spaghetti is coated all over with sauce.

5. Fold in the parsley and sprinkle with more Parmesan. Serve immediately.

INGREDIENTS

18 ounces spaghetti

Salt

4 eggs

2 ounces Parmesan cheese, freshly grated, plus more for garnish

Ground black pepper

3 tablespoons olive oil

5 ounces pancetta, diced

2 garlic cloves, minced

1 tablespoon heavy cream

¼ bunch fresh parsley, minced

DUNGENESS CRAB GRATIN

 1 HOUR   4 SERVINGS   ⊛ ★ ★

Turkey Day is celebrated in Animal Crossing once a year, on the fourth Thursday in November. To mark the occasion, the square in front of the service center is decorated, and Franklin provides visitors with a host of tasty delicacies, like pumpkin pie, his famous clam chowder—and this gratin. The ingredients you have to bring him to prepare it are obtained from the other villagers, who will also tell you a secret ingredient you can use to jazz up this recipe a bit: Dungeness crab. For those who don't live on the Pacific Ocean, where Dungeness crab is found, we've substituted crayfish, which are much easier to obtain in some areas and almost identical in flavor.

1. Preheat the oven to 400°F.

2. Grease the casserole dish with butter and arrange the potato slices in the dish like the shingles of a roof so the entire base is covered.

3. In a large bowl, whisk together the heavy cream, herb cream cheese, salt, black pepper, and nutmeg. Stir in the broccoli florets and crab or crayfish meat and spread evenly on top of the potato slices in the casserole dish. Sprinkle with the grated butter and generously sprinkle with the cheese.

4. Bake on the middle rack for about 45 minutes. If the cheese gets too dark toward the end of the cook time, cover the dish loosely with aluminum foil.

INGREDIENTS

1½ tablespoons butter, grated,
plus more to grease the pan

1¾ pounds firm, waxy potatoes,
peeled and cut into ⅛-inch slices

¾ cup plus 2 tablespoons heavy cream

3.5 ounces herb cream cheese or
Boursin cheese

1 teaspoon salt

½ teaspoon ground black pepper

½ teaspoon ground nutmeg

1 head broccoli, florets only

10 ounces Dungeness crab meat
or crayfish meat

5 ounces shredded cheese

Also required:
8-by-10-inch casserole dish

SHOYU RAMEN

 40 MINUTES, PLUS 12 HOURS TO MARINATE   4 SERVINGS   ★ ★

Ramen originated in ancient China, but it found its way into Japanese cuisine in the 19th century and went on to become a very popular dish in Japan and all over the world. There are traditionally two kinds of ramen: shoyu and miso. The flavor of miso ramen is dominated by miso, a paste made from fermented soybeans. Shoyu ramen, on the other hand, is mainly seasoned with soy sauce, which gives the finished dish a wonderful umami note. On your island, you can get this recipe at either Nook's Cranny or the Paradise Planning office in *Happy Home Paradise.* If you prefer your shoyu ramen vegetarian, simply omit the meat. And don't forget to slurp your noodles!

To make the ajitsuke tamago:

1. Put some ice cubes in a bowl of cold water.

2. Carefully poke a hole in the shell of each egg and set them in a small saucepan with enough water to cover. Bring to a boil over medium heat, then cook for 7 to 8 minutes. Use a skimmer or slotted spoon to immediately transfer the eggs to the prepared ice water.

3. While the eggs are cooling, combine the soy sauce, mirin, and water in a medium bowl, then pour into a small zip-top freezer bag.

4. Carefully shell the chilled eggs and add them to the marinade in the freezer bag. Seal the bag tightly so that the eggs are covered on all sides with marinade and refrigerate for at least 12 hours (and up to three days).

5. Remove the marinated eggs from the marinade, allow them to dry for a bit, and halve them horizontally before use.

To make the pork belly:

6. Depending on how fatty your pork belly is, use a sharp knife to cut away some of the rind and fat according to your preferences. Slice the pork belly into strips that are about 1¼ inches wide and ¾ inch thick. Place the pork belly in a large zip-top freezer bag. Add the soy sauce, chili sauce, and teriyaki sauce. Seal the bag and marinate for 2 hours in the refrigerator.

7. Transfer the pork belly and marinade to a small saucepan and stew over medium heat for 2 hours, until the pork nearly falls apart by itself.

INGREDIENTS

*For the Ajitsuke Tamago
(Marinated Ramen Eggs)*
Ice cubes

2 eggs

¼ cup soy sauce

2 tablespoons mirin

¼ cup water

For the Pork Belly
20 ounces pork belly

2 to 3 tablespoons soy sauce

2 tablespoons chili sauce

2 tablespoons teriyaki sauce

For the Broth
One 32-ounce package (4 cups)
chicken stock

2 tablespoons sake

1 tablespoon soy sauce

3.5 ounces canned bean sprouts, drained

Leaves of 1 small head bok choy

One-half 8-ounce can pickled
bamboo shoots, drained

To make the broth:

8. In a medium saucepan over medium heat, combine the chicken stock, sake, and soy sauce. Add the sprouts, bok choy, and bamboo shoots and simmer for 10 minutes, stirring gently from time to time.

To assemble:

9. Use kitchen shears to cut the nori sheet into eight equal-size squares.

10. Divide the broth and vegetables evenly among four serving bowls. Set the desired amount of pork belly on top, garnish with half an egg, and place two squares of nori decoratively on the edge of each bowl. Sprinkle with the scallions and furikake seasoning (if using). Serve immediately.

For Assembly
1 nori sheet

½ *bunch scallions, green part only, thinly sliced into rings*

Furikake seasoning (optional)

VEGGIE QUICHE

 1 HOUR & 30 MINUTES (INCL. RESTING, COOLING, AND BAKING)   **4 SERVINGS**   ★ ★

Quiche, a flat, round, pie-like dish of custard packed with vegetables inside a pie crust, is a specialty of French cuisine. For this recipe, you don't have to include the orange pumpkin used to make it on the island in AC, but you can use mini pumpkins instead if you'd like to add them to the ingredient list. This recipe ends up a little more sweet than savory, but the main thing is that it tastes great!

1. To make the dough, put the flour, salt, baking powder, vegetable oil, and water in a bowl and combine with an electric mixer or stand mixer with the kneading hook attachment for about 5 minutes or until no flour is visible. Then cover the bowl with plastic wrap and refrigerate for 20 minutes.

2. Meanwhile, to make the filling, heat the oil in a frying pan over medium heat. Add the onion and sweat until translucent. Add the vegetables and sauté on all sides for 5 minutes. Remove the pan from heat and allow to cool to room temperature.

3. Preheat the oven to 390°F.

4. Take the dough out of the refrigerator and knead it by hand for 2 minutes. Using a rolling pin, roll the dough out roughly on the work surface until you have a piece large enough to cover the base of the springform pan. The dough should no longer be sticky. It should peel readily off the work surface; if not, work in a bit more flour.

5. Grease the springform pan.

6. Place the dough in the pan and gently use your fingers to press it up the sides of the pan. Arrange the vegetables in an even layer in the pan.

7. Thoroughly whisk the cream and eggs together in a mixing bowl. Season with salt, pepper, and lovage and pour evenly over the veggies. Bake for about 30 to 35 minutes until golden brown. Then remove from the oven and allow to cool for several minutes.

8. Carefully remove from the pan before serving.

INGREDIENTS

For the Dough
2½ cups flour

1 teaspoon salt

1 teaspoon baking powder

⅓ cup plus 2 teaspoons vegetable oil

⅓ cup plus 2 tablespoons cold water

For the Filling
1 tablespoon olive oil

1 small onion, diced

20 ounces vegetables (such as zucchini, tomatoes, carrots), diced

¾ cup plus 2 tablespoons cream

3 eggs

1 teaspoon salt

½ teaspoon pepper

1 teaspoon lovage

Butter, for greasing the pan

Also required:
Springform pan (diameter about 11 inches)

POKE

 1 HOUR & 30 MINUTES (INCL. MARINATING TIME)   4 SERVINGS   ★ ★

Poke salad and bowls are huge in the culinary world right now—not just in real life, but also on the Animal Crossing islands. Once you've caught four salmon, Chip, your fishing instructor, will tell you how to use them to make this tasty poke. Poke originated in Hawaii, where it is considered something of a signature dish. It brings together very different flavors, which combine to make a spectacular meal.

To make the salmon:

1. In a small bowl, stir together the lime juice, soy sauce, black pepper, and turbinado sugar. Transfer the marinade to a large zip-top freezer bag, then add the salmon and gently massage. Refrigerate for at least 1 hour to marinate. Then pour off the marinade.

To make the rice:

2. Meanwhile, cook the sushi rice according to the instructions on the package.

3. In a small bowl, combine the rice wine vinegar, granulated sugar, and salt and stir into the cooked rice.

To make the wakame salad:

4. Wash the seaweed and combine in a medium bowl with the lime juice, sesame oil, and rice wine vinegar. Season to taste with black pepper and a bit of granulated sugar. Cover loosely with plastic wrap and refrigerate for at least 15 minutes and preferably longer for the flavors to meld. Pour off any excess liquid and stir well to combine before use.

To make the red cabbage:

5. Place the cabbage in a large bowl. Add the salt and vinegar, kneading vigorously by hand until the cabbage softens noticeably. Allow it to stand for 10 minutes for the flavors to meld. Pour off any excess liquid.

INGREDIENTS

For the Salmon
Juice of 1 lime

¼ cup soy sauce

1 teaspoon ground black pepper

1 teaspoon turbinado or raw sugar

14 ounces sashimi-quality salmon, cut into ¾-inch cubes

For the Rice
1 cup sushi rice

1 tablespoon rice wine vinegar

1 teaspoon granulated sugar

1 tablespoon salt

For the Wakame Salad
5 ounces wakame seaweed

1 teaspoon lime juice

1 tablespoon sesame oil

1 tablespoon rice wine vinegar

Ground black pepper

Granulated sugar

For the Red Cabbage
7 ounces red cabbage, thinly sliced

1 teaspoon vinegar

1 teaspoon salt

To assemble:

6. Divide the rice evenly among serving bowls and arrange the other ingredients on top, as shown.

7. Sprinkle with white and black sesame and serve immediately.

TIP OF THE DAY
To make this dish vegetarian, simply substitute smoked tofu for the salmon. Cut the tofu into bite-size cubes and sauté in a bit of oil.

For Assembly

1 avocado, pitted, peeled, and thinly sliced

1 cucumber, thinly sliced

4 radishes, thinly sliced

2 carrots, peeled and julienned

7 ounces ready-to-eat edamame

White sesame seed for garnish

Black sesame seed for garnish

PILAF

 35 MINUTES 4 SERVINGS ★ ★

Pilaf is a Middle Eastern dish made with rice, onions, broth, and meat, fish, or vegetables. It appears in Arabic texts from the 13th century, so it's been around for a while. Not much about the basic recipe has changed in all this time. The pilaf you can buy in AC, available from sources including Nook's Cranny, or as a reward in *Happy Home Paradise*, is extremely traditional. And why not? Not everything that was hip seven hundred years ago is still appealing today, but this dish definitely is!

1. Combine the rice and water in a medium saucepan. Add 1 teaspoon of salt and allow the rice to soften for 10 minutes. Then bring the rice to a boil over medium heat. Immediately cover, lower the heat to low, and simmer until the water has evaporated completely, about 15 to 20 minutes. Do not stir during this stage. Remove from the heat and add the butter, stirring until it melts and is combined thoroughly.

2. While the rice is cooking, warm the oil in a second medium saucepan over medium heat until it shimmers. Add the onion and garlic and cook until the onion is translucent, about 2 to 3 minutes. Add the lamb and cook for 6 to 8 minutes, until browned on all sides. Add the lamb broth and reduce for a few minutes. Stir in the diced tomatoes, red pepper flakes, saffron, currants, cumin, and coriander. Add salt to taste and simmer, uncovered, for 5 minutes.

3. Meanwhile, toast the pine nuts in a small dry pan over medium heat until golden brown, about 8 to 10 minutes. Remove the pine nuts from the pan, allow them to cool briefly, and finely chop them.

4. Add the cooked rice to the meat sauce, stir well to combine, and allow the mixture to stand for 2 minutes to meld the flavors. Stir in the pine nuts and garnish with parsley to serve.

INGREDIENTS

1½ cups long-grain rice

1½ cups water

Salt

2 tablespoons butter

2 tablespoons neutral oil

1 onion, diced

2 garlic cloves, minced

18 ounces lamb, cut into bite-size pieces

3⅓ cups lamb broth

7 ounces canned diced tomatoes

1 teaspoon red pepper flakes

1 envelope (125 mg) saffron threads

3 tablespoons Zante currants

1 teaspoon ground cumin

1 teaspoon ground coriander

3 tablespoons pine nuts

Chopped fresh parsley for garnish

SQUID-INK SPAGHETTI

CONTAINS ALCOHOL

 20 MINUTES   2 SERVINGS   ★

Going fishing in AC is more than just a relaxing hobby. It's also a pretty rewarding activity. Aside from the fact that this is how you get fish, which you can sell or use to make tasty foods, some of the things you catch have even more benefits. Snag a squid in your net, for example, and the idea of whipping up the recipe for this delectable Mediterranean pasta dish might come to you just as readily. Of course, catching a squid involves a fair bit of luck and a certain amount of skill with a rod, net, and bait. If you need pointers, talk to Chip, who runs the fishing tournament. He's sure to have a tip or two for you—no fish stories involved!

1. In a large pot of generously salted water, cook the spaghetti according to the package instructions until it is al dente, usually about 6 minutes. Drain the pasta in a strainer, leaving it there to drip thoroughly.

2. While the pasta is cooking, in a large skillet over medium heat, warm the oil until it shimmers. Add the squid rings and cook for 5 to 7 minutes, until brown on all sides. Lower the heat to medium, add the onions and garlic, and sauté for 2 minutes. Deglaze the skillet with the wine, then simmer for 2 to 3 minutes.

3. Add the pasta to the skillet, stir well to combine, and season generously with salt and black pepper to taste. Serve immediately, garnished with basil.

INGREDIENTS

9 ounces black (squid ink) spaghetti

Salt

2 tablespoons olive oil

10 ounces frozen squid rings, thawed

2 small onions, minced

2 garlic cloves, minced

¾ cup plus 2 tablespoons dry white wine

Ground black pepper

Fresh basil for garnish

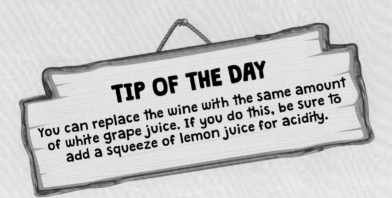

TIP OF THE DAY

You can replace the wine with the same amount of white grape juice. If you do this, be sure to add a squeeze of lemon juice for acidity.

SIDES

Animal Crossing is famous for its customization options. You can think of side dishes as options for customizing your meal. Mix and match these recipes with the others in this book to build the mealtime masterpieces you've always wanted! And don't forget to invite some neighbors over to enjoy your creations.

BAKED POTATOES

 1 HOUR & 15 MINUTES 4 SERVINGS   ★

Potatoes are a staple food in AC, and you can easily grow them yourself. You'll need seed potatoes, which you can buy from Leif. Or you can take a tour with Kapp'n and, if you're lucky, land on an island where potatoes grow. Then you can either harvest them or dig them up and plant them in your own garden at home. All you have to do then is water them regularly, and four days later, you'll have the first harvest of your very own. You can use your bounty to make these tasty baked potatoes—or just pick some up at your nearest supermarket. Either way, the recipe is the same.

1. Preheat the oven to 400°F.

2. In a small bowl, combine the sour cream, lemon juice, and goat cheese. Season the mixture generously with salt and black pepper.

3. Using a fork, prick the potatoes all over several times. Wrap each one in aluminum foil and set them on the middle rack of the oven. Position a baking sheet underneath to catch any drippings. Bake for 45 to 60 minutes, or until a knife can be inserted effortlessly. Then remove them from the oven. Careful, the potatoes will be hot!

4. Allow the potatoes to cool for several minutes. Unwrap the potatoes one at a time. Use a sharp knife to cut a large X into the top side of each, then press both sides of the potato away from the middle so the cut opens evenly. Insert generous amounts of the sour cream filling. Finally, sprinkle the chives over the top.

5. Serve immediately.

INGREDIENTS

¾ cup plus 2 tablespoons sour cream

1 tablespoon lemon juice

2 ounces goat cheese, crumbled

Salt

Ground black pepper

4 large potatoes, scrubbed and dried well

Minced fresh chives for garnish

RISOTTO

 25 MINUTES   **2 SERVINGS**   ★ ★

Risotto, originally an Italian porridge dish, has been around longer than even Graham or Cranston, hard though that may be to believe. Made from just a few simple ingredients, risotto was long viewed as a poor man's supper. And yet it is a true delicacy when prepared correctly! But preparing it correctly is the tricky part. On your island, you won't have any trouble if you get the recipe from Nook's Cranny or the Café. And in the real world, this recipe makes preparing risotto a snap!

To make the basil pesto:

1. Briefly toast the pine nuts in a small dry pan over medium heat. Remove from the heat and allow them to cool slightly.

2. Crush the pine nuts and garlic in a mortar until you have a smooth paste. (Alternatively, process with a food processor.) Add the salt and basil and crush thoroughly until a green mass forms. Now add the Parmesan and oil and stir or crush again thoroughly until a creamy paste forms. Season to taste with black pepper and possibly a bit more salt.

To make the risotto:

3. In a large saucepan over medium heat, melt 1½ tablespoons of the butter. Add the onions and sweat until translucent, about 2 to 3 minutes. Slowly stir in the rice and allow it to briefly absorb the butter, then deglaze the pan with the wine. Increase the heat to medium-high and simmer until the rice absorbs the wine, about 3 minutes. Then gradually stir in the vegetable broth over medium heat. Season to taste with salt and black pepper and cook, stirring constantly, for about 15 minutes. Shortly before the end of the cooking time, stir in the remaining 2 tablespoons of butter so the risotto gets nice and creamy.

4. Transfer the cooked risotto to plates, top with basil pesto to taste, sprinkle with a bit of freshly grated Parmesan, and serve garnished with basil.

INGREDIENTS

For the Basil Pesto
¼ cup pine nuts

1 garlic clove, minced

½ pinch salt

2 bunches fresh basil (about 1 ounce), plus more for garnish

2 ounces grated Parmesan cheese, plus more for garnish

½ cup olive oil

Pinch ground black pepper

For the Risotto
3½ tablespoons butter, divided

1 small onion, diced

¾ cup arborio rice

Scant ¼ cup dry white wine

1¾ cups vegetable broth

Pinch salt

Pinch ground black pepper

Also required:
Mortar and pestle

POTATO GALETTE

 1 HOUR & 15 MINUTES (INCL. BAKING)   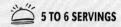 **5 TO 6 SERVINGS**   ★ ★

"Galette" is a French term for a round, flat cake made of grain or potatoes. In the game, you can get this recipe from a cooking neighbor or the chef in *Happy Home Paradise*, where you will need 2x flour and 3x potatoes to make it. That does sound like a rather—how should we put this?—*bland* meal. That's why we've added a few more ingredients for an unbeatably creamy, savory potato galette!

1. Preheat the oven to 350°F. Line a baking sheet with parchment paper.

2. Rinse the potatoes thoroughly in cold running water. Peel, then slice them very thinly (about 1 millimeter thick). Transfer to a medium bowl.

3. Add the butter and 3.5 ounces of the cheese to the bowl. Season to taste with salt, pepper, and nutmeg and combine thoroughly with a wooden spoon.

4. Using your hands, arrange the seasoned potato slices evenly in the springform pan until all the potatoes are used up. Then carefully remove the springform collar and bake on the middle rack of the oven for about 30 minutes or until golden brown. Sprinkle with the remaining cheese and continue baking for another 15 minutes.

5. Sprinkle with a bit of minced parsley to serve.

INGREDIENTS

2 pounds firm, waxy potatoes

3 tablespoons butter, melted

3.5 ounces shredded cheese, plus another 1.75 ounces

Salt, to taste

Pepper, to taste

Nutmeg, to taste

Fresh parsley, finely chopped, for garnish

Also required:
Peeler

Springform pan without base (diameter approximately 11 inches)

KETCHUP FRIED RICE

 15 MINUTES   2 SERVINGS   ★

"There's always more fish in the sea," says Punchy the cat. But what if you can't get to the sea, or the grocery store, and have to throw something together using whatever you have on hand? Necessity is the mother of invention, and sometimes the end result is delicious. This is a classic "odds and ends" kind of dish, in the most positive way: rice with ketchup—and, in this version, a few more ingredients to liven it up a bit. On your Animal Crossing island, you can get this recipe by designing a vacation home for Bam, Canberra, Cousteau, Croque, or Pekoe. While you work on that, try this recipe between AC visits.

1. In a large skillet over medium heat, warm a bit of oil until it shimmers. Add the onions and sweat until translucent, about 2 to 3 minutes. Add the carrots and sauté for 3 minutes. Add the eggs and stir well to combine, cook until the egg sets, then stir well to combine and break up the egg.

2. Place the cooked rice and a bit of oil in a separate medium skillet over medium heat. Fry, stirring frequently, until the rice is as crisp and as golden brown as you like it. Add the fried rice to the skillet with the vegetables and scrambled eggs.

3. Add the peas, corn, and ketchup, stir well to combine, and cook for a few minutes, stirring occasionally, until the peas and corn are warmed through. Season to taste with salt, black pepper, and more ketchup if desired. Serve sprinkled with a bit of parsley.

INGREDIENTS

Neutral oil for frying

1 large onion, diced

5 ounces carrots, peeled and diced

2 eggs

1 cup cooked rice
(ideally from the day before)

5 ounces canned peas, drained

3.5 ounces canned corn, drained

¼ cup tomato ketchup,
plus more as needed

Salt

1 teaspoon ground black pepper

Chopped fresh parsley for garnish

SWEETS & DESSERTS

From coconut pancakes to delicious dango, life on your Animal Crossing island is pretty sweet. What better way to bring a bit of AC into your real life than to re-create some of those sweet treats?

FRUIT SALAD

 15 MINUTES   **4 SERVINGS**   ★

Everyone knows fruit is healthy. Even so, this fruit salad is only available for special occasions in AC. One such occasion is Turkey Day, which is held every fall. On orders from Isabelle, Franklin is tasked with preparing a feast including this salad. But since Franklin can't move away from his stand while cooking, he asks you to get the vinegar, orange, apple, and beehive he needs. Of course, you can also use these very same ingredients in real life, but ultimately, Franklin's recipe—like all recipes—is just a suggestion. The best fruit salad is made with whatever fruit is on hand and in season. After all, the nicest thing about cooking is the same thing that makes Animal Crossing itself so appealing: You can give your imagination free rein!

1. In a large bowl, combine the strawberries, banana, kiwi, apple, grapes, and orange segments.

2. In a small bowl, stir together the honey, lime zest, lime juice, and sugar. Pour this mixture over the fruit and stir well to combine, making certain to coat the fruit on all sides. Allow it to stand for 5 minutes to meld the flavors, then garnish with fresh mint.

3. Arrange appealingly in a large serving bowl and serve immediately, or cover with plastic wrap and refrigerate until consumed. Stir well before enjoying.

INGREDIENTS

7 ounces fresh strawberries, tops cut off and quartered

2 bananas, peeled and thinly sliced

2 kiwi, peeled and sliced into thin wedges

1 tart apple, sliced into thin wedges

3.5 ounces seedless grapes

1 orange, peeled and segmented

1 tablespoon honey

1 teaspoon grated lime zest

3 tablespoons fresh lime juice

2 tablespoons sugar

Fresh mint for garnish

COCONUT PANCAKES

 35 MINUTES (INCL. RESTING TIME)　　 4 SERVINGS　　★ ★

Zucker loves pancakes, especially the coconut variety. Can you blame him? They're delicious and easy to make! In real life, although you need a few more ingredients, preparing these coconut pancakes is still child's play. Especially since you don't need whole coconuts, just a bit of coconut milk and some grated coconut for garnishing. And you don't have to spend hours combing the beach, hoping to find a bottle containing the recipe.

1. Place the buttermilk, vanilla, and eggs in a medium bowl. Use an electric mixer set on medium speed to beat until thoroughly combined and creamy, about 2 minutes.

2. In a separate medium bowl, combine the flour, salt, baking powder, 3.5 ounces unsweetened shredded coconut, and the sugar.

3. In a small saucepan over medium heat, melt the butter, stirring occasionally. Add the melted butter and buttermilk mixture to the flour mixture. Carefully combine and allow the batter to rest for 15 minutes.

4. In a large nonstick skillet over high heat, melt a bit of butter. Add 3 to 4 tablespoons of batter per pancake, leaving room between the cakes. (If you want your pancakes to be especially evenly shaped, use a pancake pan or a mini frying pan to make one pancake at a time.) Cook the first side for 2 to 3 minutes, until golden brown, then flip the pancake and cook the second side for another 2 minutes, until golden brown. Transfer the pancakes to paper towels on a plate to drain and cover loosely with aluminum foil to keep warm. Repeat this process with the remaining batter, adding more butter to the pan as needed.

5. Once all the pancakes have cooled slightly, place the heavy cream and condensed milk in a medium bowl. Use the electric mixer set on medium speed to combine until creamy. Stack the pancakes on a serving plate, generously pour the cream mixture over them, and garnish with the remaining shredded coconut. Serve immediately.

INGREDIENTS

1¾ cups buttermilk, at room temperature

1 teaspoon vanilla extract

2 eggs, at room temperature

2½ cups all-purpose flour

Pinch salt

3 teaspoons baking powder

5 ounces unsweetened shredded coconut, divided

¼ cup sugar

3 tablespoons butter, plus more for frying the pancakes

¾ cup plus 2 tablespoons heavy cream

One 7-ounce can sweetened condensed milk

75

POMPOMPURIN PUDDING

 3 HOURS (INCL. COOLING TIME)   6 SERVINGS   ★ ★

Does this dessert remind you of anything? That's right! The Pompompurin series, which includes everything from furniture to clothing and various knickknacks—and this pudding with the iconic Pompompurin look. In the game, this pudding can only be obtained with Pompompurin cookies—which, in turn, are only available with the appropriate amiibo cards. So getting your hands on this specific dessert isn't all that easy. But it's worth the effort! Just ask Marty, who set off to travel the entire world and try every kind of pudding in existence. Marty loves Pompompurin pudding—and he should know!

To make the pudding:

1. Set aside 6 tablespoons of the milk. Transfer the rest of the milk to a medium bowl. Add the sugar and pudding mix, stirring gently with a fork until no lumps remain, about 2 minutes.

2. Set six 5-ounce pudding molds on the counter.

3. Bring the 6 tablespoons of milk to a boil in a small saucepan over medium heat, whisking constantly. Immediately remove from the heat and carefully add the pudding mixture, stirring constantly. Return the pot to the stove and bring to a brief boil, 1 to 2 minutes, until the pudding thickens. Remove from the heat again and divide evenly among the molds. Allow them to cool at room temperature for 10 minutes, then refrigerate for at least 2 hours.

To make the cookies:

4. Meanwhile, combine the flour, baking powder, butter, sugar, vanilla, and egg in a medium bowl. Knead by hand or with an electric mixer fitted with a dough hook attachment until the dough is smooth and a bit crumbly, about 5 minutes. Wrap the dough in plastic wrap and refrigerate for 30 minutes.

5. Preheat the oven to 350°F. Line a baking sheet with parchment paper. Arrange six wooden skewers evenly on top of the paper.

6. Spread out the chilled dough on a lightly floured counter and knead vigorously by hand for 3 to 5 minutes, until the dough is nice and smooth. If the dough is still sticky, work in a bit more flour. Then roll out the dough with a rolling pin until it is a little less than ½ inch thick. Use the mouth of a 1¼- to 1½-inch glass to make six round, clearly visible impressions in the dough without cutting them out as cookies (so don't press in too deeply).

INGREDIENTS

For the Pudding
2¼ cups whole milk

¼ cup sugar

1 package vanilla pudding mix

For the Cookies
1 cup all-purpose flour, plus more for the counter

½ teaspoon baking powder

3½ tablespoons butter, at room temperature

¼ cup sugar

1 teaspoon vanilla extract

1 egg

For the Decoration
½ cup plus 4 teaspoons milk chocolate

1 brown edible marker

7 ounces mixed fresh fruit (such as strawberries, raspberries, and orange wedges)

4 ounces caramel sauce

12 store-bought meringues

Also required:
Six 5-ounce pudding molds

6 wooden skewers

Glass (diameter 1¼ to 1½ inches)

7. Then use a bread knife to draw ears and beret onto the dough and cut these features out. Lay the skewers onto the baking sheet, then lay a cookie over one end of each skewer, like lollipops. Press lightly so the cookies adhere to the skewers. Bake for 10 to 12 minutes, until golden brown. Remove the cookies from the oven and allow to cool completely on the baking sheet.

To decorate:

8. Place the chocolate in a medium bowl and melt in 10-second intervals, stirring after each. Carefully dip the beret of each cookie into the melted chocolate and allow them to set upside down. When set, remove the cookies and use the brown edible marker to draw the typical Pompompurin face onto each cookie.

9. Peel and cut the fruit into bite-size pieces as necessary.

10. Once all of the elements have been prepared—and not before!—turn the pudding out of the molds onto individual dessert plates to serve. Be sure to wait until this stage and do not unmold the pudding before then. Drizzle with caramel sauce to taste and carefully insert the skewer of one cookie into the center of each pudding. Decorate each plate with three meringues and a bit of fruit and enjoy promptly.

PEAR JELLY

 3 HOURS & 10 MINUTES (INCL. COOLING TIME)   **4 SERVINGS**   ★

For a little historical background, gelatin dessert as such was invented over 170 years ago by Peter Cooper, a child of Dutch immigrants who applied for a U.S. patent for gelatin with fruit added as a sweet dish in 1845. From there, this delicious jiggly dessert, which is known under different names all over the world, swept the globe. And at some point the recipe washed up on the shores of Animal Crossing, carried in a bottle. Preparing it is simple. It's always a safe bet whatever your cooking skills, and everyone likes gelatin desserts.

1. Set the gelatin in a small bowl and soften in cold water according to the package directions.

2. Meanwhile, bring the pear juice to a boil in a small saucepan over medium heat. Lower the heat to low, then add the sugar and maintain a simmer, stirring constantly, until the sugar has fully dissolved, about 4 to 6 minutes.

3. Carefully squeeze the softened gelatin to remove as much liquid as possible and add it to the hot pear juice, stirring until it is dissolved. Pour the mixture evenly into four 5-ounce dessert molds, seal tightly, and refrigerate for at least 3 hours to set.

4. To serve, turn the dessert out of the molds onto small serving plates, garnish each one with a few pear slices, and serve promptly.

INGREDIENTS

6 sheets gelatin
1 cup plus 5 teaspoons pear juice
3 tablespoons sugar
1 pear, sliced into thin wedges
Also required:
Four 5-ounce gelatin dessert molds

DANGO

⏱ 40 MINUTES   🍲 40 PIECES   💰 ★ ★

Dangos are a type of Japanese dumpling. But while they are enjoyed year-round in Japan, the only time you can find them in Animal Crossing is during the Autumn Moon festival. If you miss your chance to stock up on dangos at Nook's Cranny during the event, you'll have to wait 12 months for your next opportunity! If you just can't wait that long to try this traditional dessert, check out this recipe instead.

1. Combine the two kinds of rice flour in a medium bowl. Gradually add the water, stirring to combine. Add the sugar and use your hands to work the mixture into a firm, smooth dough. If the dough feels too dry, moisten your fingers and knead in a bit of water.

2. Use a knife to divide the dough into walnut-size portions, rolling each one into a ball by hand.

3. Put some cold water in a bowl and set aside.

4. Bring 2 quarts of water to a boil in a large saucepan over medium heat, then adjust the heat to maintain a simmer. Use a slotted spoon or skimmer to carefully transfer the balls to the water, leaving some distance between them. Cook until they rise to the top on their own, about 5 minutes. Then carefully remove them from the pot, briefly immerse them in the bowl of cold water, and drain them on paper towels on a plate.

5. Once all of the dangos are cooked and have cooled a bit, serve promptly at room temperature.

INGREDIENTS

⅔ cup plus 2 teaspoons sticky rice flour

⅔ cup plus 2 teaspoons rice flour

¾ cup water

3 tablespoons sugar

KEROKEROKEROPPI SNACK

 1 HOUR (INCL. COOLING TIME)   6 PIECES ⚫ ★ ★

On the Animal Crossing islands, Kerokerokeroppi cookies are like a box of chocolates: You never know what you're going to get. The Kerokerokeroppi design includes furniture, floor coverings, and a lantern. But best of all is this cute Kerokerokeroppi dessert! There's just one tiny problem: Sadly, this snack, which tastes just as sweet as it looks, is only available with the matching amiibo cards, just like all Kerokerokeroppi products—and the cards were officially phased out quite some time ago. At least now you can still access this recipe in your own kitchen!

1. Crumble the cake scraps into a medium bowl.

2. Place the chocolate in a microwave-safe bowl and melt in 10-second intervals, stirring after each. Add the chocolate to the cake scraps, then add the butter and knead thoroughly by hand for 2 to 3 minutes, until a dough that can be readily shaped forms. Divide the dough into six equal portions and roughly shape into balls. Set the cake balls on a cutting board lined with parchment paper or on a large plate and refrigerate for 30 minutes.

3. Meanwhile, knead the white fondant by hand until soft. Remove a bit of it and shape into 12 equal balls about the size of small hazelnuts. Divide the remaining white fondant in half, place each in a small bowl, and color one with the pink food coloring and one with the orange food coloring. Use a rolling pin to roll out the fondant as thin as possible on the counter. Use a ¾-inch pastry bag tip to cut out 12 pink fondant circles. Use a 1¼-inch pastry bag tip to cut out 12 orange fondant circles.

4. Combine the remaining fondant scraps and color with the black food coloring. Knead again and roll into a very thin rope. Use a small, sharp knife to cut the rope into 12 pieces, each about 1¼ inch long.

5. Knead the green fondant by hand until soft and roll out on the counter to a ¼-inch thickness.

6. Take the cake mixture out of the refrigerator. Set the six pieces some distance apart on the green fondant and use a pizza cutter or small, sharp knife to cut out a fondant circle for each piece, making sure each circle is large enough to fully cover one cake ball.

7. Carefully wrap each cake ball in green fondant. Press the seams into place lightly, and gently smooth them so the surface is as even as possible. Add the eyes, cheeks, and mouth, pressing the individual fondant pieces lightly into place, and use the remaining black fondant to create the pupils. Set the pupils on top of the eyes.

8. Enjoy promptly at room temperature.

INGREDIENTS

14 ounces cake scraps or store-bought dry pound cake of your choice

1½ cups milk chocolate

5 tablespoons butter, at room temperature

9 ounces white fondant

18 ounces green fondant

2 to 3 drops each pink, orange, and black food coloring

Also required:
¾-inch pastry bag tip
1¼-inch pastry bag tip

SONGPYEON

🕐 1 HOUR　　　🍽 4 TO 6 SERVINGS　　　⭐ ★ ★

Chuseok (literally "autumn evening"), a Korean holiday celebrated on the 15th day of the eighth lunar month, takes place once a year in Animal Crossing, just like in the real world. Families across Korea gather for the occasion to eat together and remember their ancestors. One of the most traditional foods is songpyeon, filled rice cakes typically steamed over a bed of pine needles. On your island, you can purchase songpyeon at Nook's Cranny to mark the special occasion. In real life, this recipe makes it a cinch to whip up a batch of this dessert.

1. Evenly divide the rice flour among five small bowls. Add the blueberry juice to one bowl, the raspberry juice to another, the turmeric to the third, and the matcha powder to the fourth. Color the rice flour with each addition, leaving the fifth bowl of rice flour white.

2. Add a bit of the boiling water to each bowl. It should be just enough that the rice flour can be mixed thoroughly with a fork to take on the appropriate color. Once the rice flour has cooled to the point that you can work with it easily by hand, knead each batch carefully until it has the consistency of playdough—not sticky, relatively smooth, and not crumbly. Add a bit more water as needed. Wrap each bowl of dough tightly in plastic wrap so it will not dry out. Rest them for 30 minutes.

3. Starting with the dough that has been resting the longest, use your hands to shape it into a rope about ¾ inch in diameter. Cut the rope into eight equal pieces. Shape each piece of dough into a ball and wrap in plastic wrap. Follow the same steps with the remaining batches of dough. Then allow them to rest for several minutes.

INGREDIENTS

4 cups plus 8 teaspoons rice flour

2 tablespoons blueberry juice

2 tablespoons raspberry juice

1 teaspoon ground turmeric

1 teaspoon matcha powder

1⅓ cups boiling water, or as needed

10 ounces sesame seed, toasted

5 tablespoons honey, as thin as possible

5 ounces organic pine needles, rinsed

3 teaspoons sesame oil

Also required:
3 steamer inserts (or a bamboo steamer)

4. Meanwhile, combine the sesame seed and honey in a small bowl. Place one-third of the pine needles in each steamer insert.

5. Use your fingers to press down on the songpyeon to flatten the pieces bit by bit. Top each with 1 teaspoon of the honey-sesame paste and close the dough seamlessly around the filling by twisting the ends and pulling it lengthwise a bit. Then place the songpyeon in the steamer inserts, allowing space between them.

6. Fill a saucepan or pot that is large enough to hold the steamer inserts when stacked with about 2 inches of water. Bring the water to a boil, then lower the heat to low and set the inserts over the water once the water is no longer simmering but merely steaming. Cover and steam the songpyeon for about 20 minutes, or until they are cooked through. Then brush all sides with a bit of sesame oil and serve warm or cold.

BAKED GOODS

One of the few flaws of Animal Crossing is that the game doesn't allow you to sample the delicious scents coming out of your neighbor's kitchens (yet). Baking these recipes will make up for that by filling your cooking space with irresistible aromas.

FROSTED PRETZELS

 15 MINUTES   **6 SERVINGS**   ★

Pretzels have been around since the Middle Ages. Legend has it that they were invented in 1477 by a German court baker who was told by a local lord to "bake a cake that the sun shines through three times." When the baker's wife crossed her arms over her chest, inspiration struck and the shape of the pretzel was born. In Animal Crossing, you'll also need inspiration to acquire the recipe for pretzels, by designing a vacation home for residents like Axel, Bluebear, Melba, Rilla, or Maddie.

1. Sift the powdered sugar into a medium bowl. Add the milk and stir with a fork until no lumps remain.

2. Divide the powdered sugar mixture evenly between three small bowls and color each with the food coloring: one red, one blue, and one yellow.

3. Line two baking sheets with parchment paper.

4. Dip one-third of the pretzels in the red glaze, one-third in the blue glaze, and the last third in the yellow. Then, set them on the prepared baking sheets making sure they aren't touching. Once a sheet is full, generously and evenly sprinkle it with the multicolored sprinkles and allow the pretzels to dry completely at room temperature. Repeat with the remaining pretzels.

5. Either enjoy promptly or store at room temperature in sealed containers lined with parchment paper.

INGREDIENTS

4 cups plus 6 tablespoons powdered sugar

½ cup whole milk

3 to 5 drops each red, blue, and yellow food coloring

10 ounces store-bought salted pretzels

4.5 ounces multicolored sprinkles

PULL-APART BREAD

 2 HOURS & 30 MINUTES (INCL. RISING TIME) 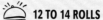 12 TO 14 ROLLS   ★ ★

What's sweet, irresistible, and a big hit at any party? No, not Fauna the fawn—pull-apart bread! (Okay, Fauna is too.) This hearty version of the popular snack is basically a sheet of dough rolled out thin and then layered to make many little pieces to tear off as desired—perfect for sharing with your friends, on your island or in real life!

1. Place the milk in a large bowl. Add the sugar and yeast, stir with a fork to combine, then cover with a clean kitchen towel and allow the mixture to stand for 10 minutes.

2. Add the salt, melted butter, and flour to the milk mixture. Using an electric mixer or stand mixer fitted with a dough hook attachment, mix on medium speed until a soft, easily shaped dough forms, about 3 to 4 minutes. Add more flour as needed. Cover the bowl with a clean dish cloth and leave to rise for at least 1 hour, or until the dough has doubled in size.

3. Grease two 11-inch springform pans on all sides with butter and line the bases with parchment paper.

4. Transfer the dough to the counter and use your thumb and forefinger to pinch off pieces that are about the size of small apples. Use your hands to shape the pieces into balls. Then arrange the balls, a finger's width apart, evenly in the prepared springform pans so each pan is completely filled with rolls (about six to seven per pan). Cover with a clean dish cloth again and leave to stand for another 20 to 30 minutes, or until the rolls have significantly increased in volume again.

5. Meanwhile, preheat the oven to 400°F.

6. One at a time, bake each springform pan on the middle rack for 18 to 20 minutes, or until the rolls are soft and fluffy. Remove them from the oven and from the pan. Allow them to cool briefly. This bread is best enjoyed while still warm.

INGREDIENTS

2¼ cups whole milk, warm

1 teaspoon sugar

1 cube fresh yeast

1 tablespoon salt

½ cup (1 stick) plus ½ tablespoon butter, melted, plus more to grease the pans

6⅔ cups all-purpose flour, plus more as needed

Also required:
Two 11-inch springform pans

CHOCOLATE HEART

CONTAINS ALCOHOL

 1 HOUR & 30 MINUTES (INCL. COOLING TIME)   4 TO 5 SERVINGS   ★ ★

Anyone who has even the slightest romantic bone in their body knows what happens on February 14. It's Valentine's Day, the day when we celebrate romantic love. If you love someone, that's when you give them your heart—preferably made out of chocolate. In the game, this gesture of affection has quite an effect on relations between characters, and in real life, too, this chocolate heart is sure to strike the right chord when you present it to your beloved. After all, what better way to prove your love than by voluntarily sharing something this delicious?

1. Preheat the oven to 350°F. Grease a 10-inch heart-shaped cake pan with butter.

2. Place the eggs, sugar, vanilla, melted chocolate, and butter in a large bowl. Use an electric mixer set on medium speed to beat until creamy, about 5 minutes. Then add the liqueur, flour, baking powder, and cocoa powder and stir to combine.

3. In a separate medium bowl, use the electric mixer on medium speed to whip the egg whites until stiff peaks form, about 4 to 5 minutes. Use a spatula to carefully fold the whipped whites into the chocolate-flour mixture. Combine thoroughly.

4. Spread the batter evenly in the prepared pan, smooth the top, and bake on the middle rack for 40 to 50 minutes, or until a toothpick inserted into the center of the cake comes out clean. Then remove the cake from the oven and leave it in the pan to cool completely.

5. Carefully remove the cooled cake from the pan and cover evenly with chocolate frosting on all sides. Smooth with a baking spatula.

6. Shape a bow and a piece of ribbon out of the red fondant. Decorate the cake with the ribbon and bow to give your loved ones a sweet surprise!

INGREDIENTS

7 tablespoons butter, at room temperature, plus more for the pan

2 eggs

½ cup sugar

1 tablespoon vanilla extract

3.5 ounces dark chocolate, melted

5 ounces coffee or hazelnut liqueur

1½ cups all-purpose flour

1 heaping tablespoon baking powder

2 teaspoons cocoa powder

2 egg whites

7 ounces store-bought chocolate cake frosting or ganache

7 ounces red fondant

Also required:
10-inch heart-shaped cake pan

TIP OF THE DAY

The coffee or hazelnut liqueur in this recipe can be replaced with an equal amount of milk.

BÛCHE DE NOËL

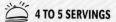 1 HOUR & 15 MINUTES   4 TO 5 SERVINGS   ★ ★ ★

Bûche de Noël ("Yule log") is a traditional Christmas pastry from France and other Francophone countries, where it is served as a holiday dessert. The first official mention of bûche de Noël was in 1879. This cake is divinely delicious, and it sure doesn't taste a bit like the fallen log that inspired the recipe. Some of the Animal Crossing residents, like Alfonso, Jitters, Bluebear, Carmen, Daisy, and Ellie, will give you a Yule log as thanks if you help them out with their vacation home construction projects. Admittedly, preparing this dish isn't exactly simple, and it does take some time. But all the effort is worthwhile any time of year.

1. Preheat the oven to 350°F. Line a baking sheet with parchment paper.

2. Separate the eggs, placing the whites in one medium bowl and the yolks in another medium bowl. Use an electric mixer set on medium speed to beat the egg whites until stiff peaks form, about 4 to 5 minutes. Gradually add the sugar and vanilla and combine until the egg white mixture is completely stiff and nicely glossy, about 5 minutes.

3. Use the electric mixer set on medium speed to beat the egg yolks until they are creamy, very light in color, and doubled in bulk. Then carefully fold the egg white mixture into the yolk mixture.

4. In a separate medium bowl, combine the flour, baking powder, cornstarch, and cocoa powder. Sift this mixture over the egg mixture, then fold in. Spread the mixture over the prepared baking sheet and bake for 12 to 15 minutes.

5. Set a clean kitchen towel that's the size of the baking sheet on the counter and carefully turn out the still-hot chocolate sponge cake on top of the towel and remove the parchment paper if it has stuck. Using the towel to manipulate the cake, roll up the cake like a carpet, into a log shape about the thickness of your arm. Allow it to cool completely in the rolled position at room temperature.

INGREDIENTS

4 eggs

½ cup sugar

1 teaspoon vanilla extract

½ cup plus 4 teaspoons all-purpose flour

1 teaspoon baking powder

¼ cup cornstarch

⅓ cup cocoa powder

¾ cup plus 2 tablespoons heavy cream

1 cup plus 3 tablespoons coarsely chopped chocolate chips or semisweet baking chocolate

14 ounces hazelnut cocoa spread

Mixed fresh fruit (such as strawberries, blueberries) for garnish

Store-bought green decorative fondant leaves for garnish

6. Meanwhile, bring the heavy cream to a boil in a small saucepan over medium heat. Immediately remove from the heat, add the chocolate, and stir frequently until the chocolate has melted completely. Transfer the mixture to a bowl. Whisk repeatedly until the ganache starts to firm up to the point that it can be spread.

7. Carefully unroll the fully cooled sponge cake and spread an even, generous layer of hazelnut cocoa spread over the top. Then use the dish towel to roll up the sponge cake again. Using a large, sharp knife, slice off one end. Set this piece on top of the roll.

8. Carefully set the cake on a serving plate large enough to hold it and coat generously on all sides with the ganache. Don't worry about being too precise. Use a fork to scratch the ganache lengthwise along the sides of the cake so it looks like a log. Garnish with the fresh fruit and fondant leaves to taste.

9. Cover loosely with plastic wrap and refrigerate until served.

APPLE PIE

 1 HOUR & 30 MINUTES (INCL. COOLING TIME) 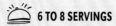 6 TO 8 SERVINGS   ★ ★

"You snooze, you lose," lazy villager Beau likes to say. But he'd better make sure he's up and about when this apple pie gets made! Otherwise, he won't get a single slice. The wonderful thing about apple pie is that it can be adjusted to suit any taste. You can make it however you like, which means there are many different versions out there. But all of them share one trait: They're delicious! Here's the recipe for the classic American version, just like the one you'll find in Animal Crossing.

To make the shortbread dough:

1. Combine the flour and baking powder in a small bowl, then sift into a large bowl. Spread the butter evenly over the flour mixture. Add the granulated sugar, vanilla, and egg and knead vigorously by hand until a smooth, supple dough forms. Cover the bowl with plastic wrap and refrigerate for 30 minutes.

2. Grease an 8- or 9-inch pie pan or deep tart pan with butter.

3. Flour the counter. Take the dough out of the refrigerator and knead by hand for a few minutes, until the dough no longer crumbles or sticks to your fingers. Then divide it into two equal portions and use a rolling pin to roll each one out to about a ½-inch thickness. Place one of the dough circles in the prepared pan and press into place all around and on the base of the pan. Using your hands, carefully pull the dough up the sides of the pan, then cut off any excess at the top of the pan. Prick the base all over with a fork.

4. Slice the second circle of dough into ½-inch-thick strips.

5. Preheat the oven to 350°F.

To make the filling:

6. Combine the margarine, granulated sugar, cinnamon, eggs, vanilla, flour, and baking powder. Use an electric mixer set on medium speed to beat for 2 to 3 minutes, until a smooth batter forms. Carefully fold in the apples.

To assemble:

7. Fill the dough-lined pan evenly with apple filling, then smooth the top. Use the strips of dough to form a lattice pattern on the counter. Place the lattice evenly on top of the entire pie. Press into place at the edges and cut off all excess. Brush the lattice with the egg yolk, then bake for 25 to 30 minutes, or until a toothpick inserted into the center comes out clean.

8. Remove the pie from the oven and allow it to cool completely in the pan. Sprinkle with powdered sugar as desired before serving.

INGREDIENTS

For the Shortbread Dough

1½ cups all-purpose flour, plus more for the counter

1 teaspoon baking powder

5 tablespoons cold butter or margarine, cut into ½-inch cubes, plus more to grease the pan

⅜ cup granulated sugar

1 tablespoon vanilla extract

1 egg

For the Filling

1 cup (2 sticks) margarine

1 cup granulated sugar

Pinch ground cinnamon

5 eggs

1 tablespoon vanilla extract

3 cups all-purpose flour

1 rounded tablespoon baking powder

3 large apples, peeled, cored, and cut into 1-inch cubes

For Assembly

1 egg yolk, beaten

Powdered sugar for sprinkling

Also required:

8- or 9-inch pie pan or deep tart pan

CAKE SALÉ

 2 HOURS & 20 MINUTES (INCL. RISING TIME)    6 TO 8 SERVINGS   ★ ★

You might not think the combination of "salt" and "cake" sounds very appetizing at first. Fair enough! But this baked item—which is actually more bread than cake—is highly versatile when it comes to ingredients, and you can use almost anything you happen to have handy. What's in season on your island right now? Carrots? Toss them in! Potatoes? Of course! Pumpkin? Have at it! Just make sure to use savory ingredients if at all possible, because as the name suggests, this dish features a powerful salty flavor, and although we wouldn't want to hamper your creativity, salt and fruit don't go together very well. But vegetables are always a great choice!

1. In a small bowl, combine the yeast and water and stir with a fork.

2. Place the flour in a medium bowl and add the salt. Add the dissolved yeast and butter. Using an electric mixer fitted with a dough hook attachment, combine by starting on a low setting and gradually increasing the speed until a smooth dough forms, about 5 minutes.

3. Preheat the oven to 125°F, then turn it off. Cover the dough with a clean dish cloth and set it in the oven to rise for 30 minutes, or until the dough has visibly increased in volume.

4. Meanwhile, combine the sun-dried tomatoes, leek, and pancetta in a small bowl and set aside.

5. Transfer the risen dough to a floured surface and knead vigorously by hand for 3 to 4 minutes, working the tomato mixture into the dough in batches. Roughly shape the dough into a long "brick," set it in a 10-by-5-inch loaf pan, and press lightly into place on all sides. Cover with a clean dish cloth and allow the dough to rise for another 40 to 45 minutes, or until it has noticeably increased in size again.

6. Meanwhile, preheat the oven to 375°F.

7. Bake the bread for 40 to 45 minutes. Then remove it from the oven, allow it to cool for several minutes, and carefully remove it from the pan. It is best enjoyed warm.

INGREDIENTS

1 cube fresh yeast

1⅓ cups water, lukewarm

4 cups plus 2 tablespoons all-purpose flour, plus more for the counter

1½ teaspoons salt

2 teaspoons butter, at room temperature

One 7-ounce jar sun-dried tomatoes, minced

1 small leek, minced

3.5 ounces pancetta

Also required:
10-by-5-inch loaf pan

CARROT CAKE

 1 HOUR & 30 MINUTES (INCL. COOLING TIME)   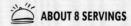 ABOUT 8 SERVINGS   ★ ★

Some people consider carrots as "healthy food," to be used mainly in salads and soups. But carrots have a place on the dessert menu too. Especially when made into a delectably sweet, moist cake topped with a healthy dollop of whipped cream! Dotty, Doc, and Coco would undoubtably agree.

1. Preheat the oven to 350°F. Generously grease a 9-inch springform pan with butter.

To make the cake:

2. In a medium bowl, combine the eggs, granulated sugar, oil, and cinnamon. Use an electric mixer set on medium speed to beat until smooth, 3 to 4 minutes. Add the carrots and ground almonds and carefully mix to combine.

3. Combine the flour and baking powder in a separate medium bowl. Add this flour mixture to the carrot mixture and carefully combine with the electric mixer until a smooth but still runny batter forms.

4. Transfer the batter to the prepared pan and bake for 40 to 50 minutes, or until a toothpick inserted into the middle of the cake comes out clean. Remove the cake from the oven and leave it in the pan to cool completely. Carefully remove it from the pan after that.

To decorate:

5. While the cake is cooling, place the cream cheese, powdered sugar, vanilla, and lemon juice in a medium bowl. Use an electric mixer on medium speed to combine thoroughly. Spread the frosting evenly over the cooled cake, smooth with a spatula on all sides, and allow it to dry briefly. Garnish as desired with sugar carrots.

INGREDIENTS

For the Cake
Butter for greasing the pan
4 eggs
1 cup granulated sugar
1¼ cups neutral oil
1 teaspoon ground cinnamon
14 ounces carrots, grated
2 cups ground almonds
2 cups plus 4 teaspoons all-purpose flour
2 teaspoons baking powder

For the Decoration
10 ounces cream cheese
1 cup powdered sugar
1 tablespoon vanilla extract
1 tablespoon lemon juice
Store-bought decorative sugar or marzipan carrots for garnish

Also required:
9-inch springform pan
Baking spatula

THUMBPRINT JAM COOKIES

 1 HOUR (INCL. COOLING TIME)   40 COOKIES   ★ ★

Marina might be really lazy, but if there's one thing that will get her up and moving, it's baking! And she's really good at it. Thumbprint jam cookies are her specialty. If there are two things that *everyone* likes, it's cookies and jam. So what could be more natural than putting them together? That's just what Marina did with these tasty treats, which should earn her honorary citizen status in Animal Crossing—an award you, too, can win just by whipping up a batch and sharing them. And in real life, sharing these with friends will definitely score you lots of points.

1. In a large bowl, combine the flour, baking powder, sugar, vanilla, egg, ground almonds, salt, and butter. Knead thoroughly by hand for about 10 minutes, or until a nice dough that sticks together well has formed. Wrap tightly in plastic wrap and refrigerate for at least 30 minutes.

2. Preheat the oven to 350°F. Line two baking sheets with parchment paper.

3. Vigorously knead the chilled dough again by hand. Remove small portions of dough and shape them into walnut-size balls (you should get about 40 pieces). Place the dough balls about 1 inch apart on the prepared baking sheets. Pinch one end of each ball a bit while pressing in with one finger on the opposite side to form a heart. Use the end of a wooden spoon or one thumb to create a hollow in the middle of each cookie. Using a teaspoon, fill the hollows evenly with the jam. Fill half the cookies with strawberry jam and half with apricot.

4. Bake the cookies on the two most central racks (or bake one sheet at a time on the middle rack) for 12 to 15 minutes, or until golden brown. Remove the cookies from the oven and allow them to cool for several minutes before enjoying. Store in a sealed airtight container.

INGREDIENTS

2 cups plus 4 teaspoons all-purpose flour, plus more for the counter

1 teaspoon baking powder

¾ cup sugar

1 teaspoon vanilla extract

1 egg

5 ounces ground almonds

Pinch salt

½ cup (1 stick) plus 1 tablespoon butter

3.5 ounces strawberry jam

3.5 ounces apricot jam

FRUIT SCONES

 40 MINUTES   24 SCONES   ★ ★

Pekoe the bear cub loves to paint, draw, read—and bake. And what baked good goes better with such relaxing pastimes than scones, the traditional British teatime treat? While scones are traditionally enjoyed warm with butter, jam, or honey in the UK, versions with clotted cream and grated cheddar cheese can be found as far away as South America. On the Animal Crossing islands, where you can get this recipe from the restaurant cook in *Happy Home Paradise*, classic fruit scones are especially popular.

1. Place the cranberries in a small bowl and pour boiling water over them, ensuring that the berries are completely covered. Allow them to stand for 10 minutes.

2. Meanwhile, sift the flour, baking powder, and salt into a medium bowl, holding the sifter as high above the bowl as possible to incorporate more air into the flour. Add the cold butter and, using your fingertips, work it into the flour mixture until it resembles coarse meal. Continue until no lumps of butter remain. Then add the sugar.

3. Beat the eggs in a measuring cup, then remove one-fifth of the eggs and set aside in a small bowl. Then fill the cup to the 10-ounce line with milk and stir, so you have 10 ounces of a milk-and-egg mixture.

4. Preheat the oven to 400°F. Line a baking sheet with parchment paper.

INGREDIENTS

3.5 ounces dried cranberries

3¾ cups all-purpose flour, plus more for the counter

4 teaspoons baking powder

1 teaspoon salt

7 tablespoons cold butter, cut into pieces

½ cup sugar

2 eggs

1 cup plus 2 tablespoons whole milk

Also required:
4-inch round cookie cutter

5. Drain the cranberries well and add them to the flour mixture. Add the egg mixture and use a fork to mix it into the flour mixture—this is important; you should avoid touching the dough with your hands at all. It is sufficient to press it together loosely. Under no circumstances should this dough be kneaded. The dough should not be sticky or crumbly, so add a bit of flour or milk as needed.

6. Flour the counter and use a rolling pin to carefully roll out the dough to a 1¼- to 1½-inch thickness, making sure the dough stays as light and loose as possible during this stage as well. Use a 4-inch round cookie cutter or the top of a glass to cut out rounds of dough.

7. Set the dough pieces about 1 inch apart on the prepared baking sheet. Brush them with the reserved egg and bake for 10 to 12 minutes, until golden brown. These scones are best enjoyed when warm.

ORANGE PIE

 2 HOUR & 20 MINUTES (PLUS 8 HOURS TO COOL)   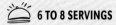 6 TO 8 SERVINGS   ★ ★

All kinds of fruit and vegetables grow on your Animal Crossing island, including oranges. You can enjoy them on their own, sell them, or use them to make tasty dishes like this orange pie—as long as you have the recipe, that is. Eating orange pie in the game will give you an energy point. In real life, you might find yourself simply delighted that this pie is so tasty. In fact, it's so delicious you might want to keep it all to yourself. Which you would never do, of course. Would you?

To make the shortbread dough:

1. In a large bowl, combine the flour, baking powder, egg, sugar, and butter. Using an electric mixer with a dough hook attachment, mix on medium speed until a smooth dough forms, 3 to 4 minutes. Divide the dough in half.

2. Grease an 11-inch springform pan with butter. Using a rolling pin, roll out half of the dough on a lightly floured surface until you have a round disk large enough to cover the base of the pan. Set the round inside the pan. Roll out the rest of the dough into a long oblong shape and press it into place along the sides of the pan, being sure the dough connects at the edges and base and is as equally thick as possible.

3. Preheat the oven to 350°F.

To make the filling:

4. In a large bowl, combine the sugar, oil, eggs, milk, vanilla, pudding mix, and yogurt. Using an electric mixer set on medium speed, combine until a smooth but very liquid mass forms. The mixture should spread out almost by itself when poured into the pan. Smooth the top slightly and bake for 1 hour. If the pie crust begins to darken too much during baking, cover it loosely with aluminum foil.

5. Turn off the oven at the end of the bake time and allow the pie to stand in the oven for at least 8 hours and ideally overnight; insert the handle of a wooden spoon into the oven door so the pie can cool slowly without cracking.

To assemble:

6. Wash the oranges and pat dry with paper towels. Peel and cut them horizontally into ¾-inch-thick slices. Prepare the glaze according to the package instructions.

7. Arrange the orange slices evenly over the top of the pie, cover with the glaze, and allow the cake to stand for about 10 minutes, or until the glaze is firm enough to cut. Then either serve the pie promptly or refrigerate it until you're ready to enjoy.

INGREDIENTS

For the Shortbread Dough
1⅔ cups all-purpose flour, plus more for the counter

1½ teaspoons baking powder

1 egg

⅜ cup sugar

5 tablespoons butter, plus more for the pan

For the Filling
1 cup sugar

½ cup neutral oil

4 eggs

2¼ cups whole milk

1 tablespoon vanilla extract

1 package vanilla pudding mix

2 pounds plain Greek yogurt

For Assembly
2 oranges

Store-bought clear cake glaze

Also required:
11-inch springform pan

BIRTHDAY CAKE

 1 HOUR & 40 MINUTES (INCL. COOLING TIME) 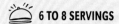 **6 TO 8 SERVINGS**   ★ ★

In Animal Crossing, on your birthday you'll be invited to a small surprise party at your favorite neighbor's house, complete with presents and a delicious birthday cake. Which cake you'll find waiting for you is a matter of chance. With this recipe, though, you know ahead of time what you're getting: a rich and impressive cake, featuring a thick layer of chocolate buttercream and strawberries, so sweet that Merengue—who always wanted to be a pastry chef—would stop at nothing to get the recipe. And let's hope she gets it, because then she can bake this delectable cake anytime, not just for birthdays.

1. Preheat the oven to 300°F. Line an 11-inch springform pan with parchment paper.

To make the cake:

2. In a medium heatproof bowl, combine the chocolate and butter. Fill a medium saucepan halfway with water and bring to a simmer. Adjust the heat to low and place the bowl on top of the pan, making sure the bottom does not touch the water. Melt the chocolate, stirring constantly to fully combine with the butter. Remove from the heat.

3. Add the sugar and vanilla and stir until the mixture has formed a smooth homogeneous mass. Allow the mixture to cool briefly.

4. Meanwhile, separate the eggs. In a medium bowl, use an electric mixer set on medium speed to beat the egg whites until stiff peaks form, about 5 minutes. Add the egg yolks, one at a time, to the chocolate mixture. Follow the same procedure with the flour. Finally, use a spatula or whisk to carefully fold in the egg whites.

5. Fill the prepared pan evenly with the batter. Smooth the top and bake on the middle rack for 40 to 45 minutes. Don't worry if the cake still seems a bit mushy—it should! This will ensure it is light and moist after cooling. Remove the cake from the oven and leave in the pan to cool completely.

To decorate:

6. Meanwhile, in a mixing cup, use an electric mixer set on medium speed to whip the heavy cream until stiff peaks form. Carefully fold in the melted (but not hot!) chocolate.

7. Transfer 6 tablespoons of the frosting to a pastry bag (alternatively, use a zip-top freezer bag with one corner cut off). Frost the cake evenly on all sides with the remaining frosting, then use the pastry bag to dot five rosettes onto the top of the cake. Garnish each one with a strawberry. Refrigerate until served.

INGREDIENTS

For the Cake
2 cups milk chocolate

¾ cup (1½ sticks) butter, at room temperature

¾ cup plus 1 tablespoon sugar

1 teaspoon vanilla extract

5 eggs

⅜ cup plus 2 teaspoons all-purpose flour

For the Decoration
¾ cup plus 2 tablespoons heavy cream

1¾ cups milk chocolate, melted

5 fresh strawberries

Also required:
11-inch springform pan

Pastry bag (optional)

Birthday candles (optional)

SNACK BREAD

 3 HOURS (INCL. RISING TIME)   8 ROLLS   ★ ★

What could be finer than getting together with family and/or good friends? How about a *picnic* with family and/or good friends, with everyone bringing something along to share? Next time you're picnicking, bring along a basket of this savory snack bread for everyone to enjoy. It's perfect for any social gathering, whether on your island or in a friend's backyard.

To make the rolls:

1. Combine the lukewarm water, milk, and sugar in a large bowl. Crumble the yeast into the bowl. Stir well to combine and allow the mixture to stand for 10 minutes. Add the flour, salt, egg, and melted butter. Using an electric mixer fitted with a dough hook attachment, mix on high speed until a smooth dough forms, about 5 minutes. Cover with a clean kitchen towel and allow the dough to stand in a warm place for 1 hour.

2. Line a baking sheet with parchment paper.

3. Divide the dough into eight equal portions. Knead two of the pieces of dough with the grated cheese and shape them into rolls. Knead two others with the hazelnut cocoa spread and shape them into rolls. Press the chocolate bars into the center of two more pieces of dough and shape them into oblong loaves. Knead the dried fruit into two of the pieces of dough and shape them into rolls. Set the rolls on the prepared baking sheet. Cover again with a clean kitchen towel and allow them to stand for 1 more hour.

To make the glaze:

4. Use a fork to combine the egg and water in a small cup.

5. Preheat the oven to 400°F.

6. Brush the tops of the rolls with the egg wash and bake on the middle rack for 16 to 20 minutes. Then remove from the oven.

To assemble:

7. Immediately sprinkle grated cheese over the cheese rolls while still hot. Place two dried orange slices on the top of each of the dried fruit rolls, moistening the rolls with a bit of water as needed so that the slices stick. Finally, use the chocolate icing to draw cute faces on the rolls containing the chocolate bars.

8. Allow the rolls to cool completely before consuming.

INGREDIENTS

For the Rolls
¾ cup plus 2 tablespoons water, lukewarm

¼ cup whole milk

3 tablespoons sugar

1 cube fresh yeast

4 cups plus 2 tablespoons all-purpose flour

1½ teaspoons salt

1 egg

6 tablespoons butter, melted

2 ounces grated cheese of your choice

2 ounces hazelnut cocoa spread

2 chocolate bars

2 ounces mixed dried fruit (such as oranges and apricots), coarsely chopped

For the Glaze
1 egg

2 tablespoons water

For Assembly
1 tablespoon grated cheese of your choice

4 dried orange slices

1 tube store-bought chocolate writing icing

MOON CAKES

 4 HOURS (INCL. CHILLING TIME) **20 PIECES** ★ ★

In some regions of Asia, Tsukimi, the annual full moon or harvest moon festival, has been celebrated on the 15th day of the eighth month of the lunisolar calendar since the late 16th century. Common customs include visiting shrines, burning incense, and making offerings like these symbol-bedecked moon cakes, which people hope will bring long life, harmony, and other good things. However, baking your own moon cakes is rare; instead, people buy them from a bakery or store. The same is true on the Animal Crossing islands, where you can get these tasty cakes filled with sweet red bean paste on the Nook Shopping app during the Autumn Moon festival. But you can bake moon cakes of your own. In fact, once you get the hang of it, preparing them with this recipe is easy!

1. Place the syrup and oil in a medium bowl. Use an electric mixer set on high speed to beat until thoroughly combined, 1 to 2 minutes. Add the vanilla and flour and continue beating until a crumbly dough forms. Then knead by hand until the dough is smooth and supple. Refrigerate for at least 3 hours.

2. In a medium skillet over medium heat, sauté the bean paste, stirring frequently, until it is very dry and has taken on the consistency of thick mashed potatoes, about 10 to 12 minutes. Then remove from the heat and allow it to cool until you can work with it by hand.

3. Lightly moisten your hands and pinch off lumps of bean paste about the size of a walnut, shaping them into 1-ounce balls. Set the balls on a plate, loosely cover with plastic wrap, and refrigerate.

4. Shape the chilled dough into ½-ounce balls. Then lightly flour your hands and roll out each dough ball on the counter until you have a round of dough as thin as possible. Set a ball of bean paste in the center of each round. Carefully pull the dough over the filling, using your judgment and patience, until the filling is completely covered. Roll into a ball between your hands.

INGREDIENTS

*2.5 ounces golden syrup,
as thick as possible*

1 teaspoon sunflower oil

2 tablespoons vanilla extract

*¾ cup plus 4 teaspoons all-purpose flour,
plus a bit more for your hands and the pan*

*17 ounces store-bought sweet
red bean paste*

1 egg

1 teaspoon water

Also required:
Moon cake pan

5. Preheat the oven to 350°F. Line a baking sheet with parchment paper.

6. Use a lightly floured moon cake pan to shape the balls, one at a time, into the typical moon cake shape and give them your desired pattern. Set the cakes on the prepared baking sheet and spray them evenly with water to prevent the dough from cracking or crumbling. Bake on the middle rack for 10 minutes.

7. Remove the moon cakes from the oven and allow them to cool on the baking sheet for 25 minutes.

8. Mix together the egg and water in a small bowl and evenly coat the tops of the moon cakes with the mixture. Then bake again at 350°F for about 20 minutes, or until the tops of the moon cakes are firm. Finally, remove the moon cakes from the oven and allow them to cool completely.

9. Best stored in a sealed container for three days before serving. This gives the moon cakes time to soften, which is how they should be consumed.

SURICHWI TTEOK

 40 MINUTES   **16 PIECES**   ★ ★

These rice cakes, a traditional Korean snack, provide a fresh burst of energy! Of course, don't expect to be pulling up trees or breaking rocks with your bare hands after eating them. Sadly, that's only possible in Animal Crossing. But unlike Animal Crossing, in the real world surichwi tteok are available anytime, not just during the Dano Festival.

1. In a medium bowl, combine the rice flour, salt, and matcha powder. Pour the boiling water over the dry mixture and stir with a wooden spoon until the mixture has cooled to the point that you can work with it by hand. Knead thoroughly for 2 minutes.

2. Divide the dough into 16 equal pieces and shape them into balls. Use the palms of your hands to gently press them flat on the counter, then stamp them with a cookie stamp. In the end, the surichwi tteok should all be round and a little less than ½ inch thick. Carefully place them some distance apart in a steamer insert.

3. Fill a medium saucepan with about 2 inches of water and bring to a boil over medium heat. Lower the heat to the lowest setting. Set the steamer insert inside the saucepan, being careful to keep it above the water. Cover and steam for about 20 minutes, or until the surichwi tteok are cooked and firm but still a bit sticky.

4. Brush them on all sides with a bit of sesame oil and enjoy immediately.

INGREDIENTS

2½ cups rice flour

1 teaspoon salt

1 teaspoon matcha powder

¾ cup boiling water

1 tablespoon sesame oil

Also required:

Cookie stamp (flower pattern, for example)

Steamer insert for cooking pot

SPOOKY COOKIES

 1 HOUR & 30 MINUTES (INCL. STANDING TIME)   30 PIECES   ★ ★

These cookies aren't just spooky, they're delicious. Not to mention delightful, just like AC's Jack, the Czar of Halloween! Speaking of Jack, Halloween jack-o'-lanterns were originally carved out of turnips. But Irish immigrants who came to the United States in the 19th century found that pumpkins were more available, and made bigger faces too! The result is the familiar Halloween tradition we know today. Can you imagine Jack with the head of a turnip?

1. Sift the flour and baking powder into a medium bowl. Add the granulated sugar, vanilla, almond extract, butter, and eggs. Using an electric mixer or stand mixer fitted with a dough hook attachment, mix on medium speed until coarsely combined, about 5 minutes. Then turn out the dough on a floured surface and knead vigorously by hand for 5 minutes. Return the dough to the bowl, cover with plastic wrap, and refrigerate for at least 30 minutes.

2. Toward the end of this time, preheat the oven to 350°F. Line two baking sheets with parchment paper.

3. Remove the dough from the refrigerator and knead briefly and thoroughly by hand again, then use a rolling pin to roll it out to a ⅜-inch thickness. Use various Halloween cookie cutters to cut out spooky shapes and set the cookies about 1 inch apart on the prepared baking sheets.

4. Bake for 10 to 12 minutes, or until the cookies are as browned as you like them. Remove the cookies from the oven and transfer them to a wire rack or clean kitchen towel to cool completely. Repeat this process until all the dough is used.

5. In a medium bowl, combine the powdered sugar and water until no lumps remain. Divide the glaze evenly among three small bowls and use the food coloring to color each one differently. Melt the chocolate in a microwave-safe bowl in 10-second intervals, stirring after each. Then dip the cookies in the glaze and chocolate as desired so they are coated on all sides. Allow them to dry briefly on a large serving plate, then use the chocolate writing icing to decorate.

6. Store in a sealed airtight container lined with parchment paper.

INGREDIENTS

4 cups plus 2 tablespoons all-purpose flour, plus more for the counter

2 teaspoons baking powder

¾ cup granulated sugar

1 teaspoon vanilla extract

2 to 3 drops almond extract

1 cup (2 sticks) plus 2 tablespoons cold butter, cut into pieces

2 eggs

4 cups plus 6 tablespoons powdered sugar

½ cup cold water

2 to 3 drops each green, yellow, and orange food coloring

½ cup plus 4 teaspoons milk chocolate

1 tube store-bought milk chocolate writing icing

Also required:
Various Halloween cookie cutters as desired

MOM'S HOMEMADE CAKE

 3 HOURS (INCL. CHILLING TIME)    6 TO 8 SERVINGS   ★ ★

In Animal Crossing, you can always count on Mom to send you a homemade cake when your birthday rolls around. What kind of cake you get depends on a number of factors, including where you live in real life. We decided on a version with strawberries and flowers here, with a generous amount of buttercream and, that's right, strawberries that look like flowers. We're certain Mom would approve!

1. Finely crumble the cookies by hand in a medium bowl. Add the almonds and melted butter, stirring to combine. Spread the mixture evenly on the base of a 9-inch springform pan, press lightly into place, and refrigerate.

2. Reserve three especially pretty strawberries to use as garnish. Slice the rest of the strawberries crosswise with a small, sharp knife.

3. In a separate medium bowl, combine the cream cheese, sour cream, sugar, and vanilla. Use an electric mixer set on medium speed to beat until creamy, 2 to 3 minutes.

4. In another medium bowl, whip the heavy cream with the electric mixer set on medium speed until stiff peaks form, about 3 to 5 minutes. Use a spatula to carefully fold the whipped cream into the cream cheese mixture. Do not stir!

5. Prepare the red cake glaze according to the package instructions and set aside.

6. Take the chilled cake base out of the refrigerator. Arrange the strawberry slices in an even layer on top of the base. Place more slices of strawberry tightly together along the edge of the pan and press lightly to adhere. Place the filling in the middle of the pan and spread evenly up to the strawberries, then smooth the top. Carefully pour the cake glaze over the filling, smoothing outward to the edge, and leave an X free of glaze in three spots so the final product will look just like it does in Animal Crossing.

7. Garnish with the three reserved strawberries, cover the pan loosely with plastic wrap, and refrigerate for at least 2 hours to set. Carefully remove the cake from the pan after that, and enjoy slightly chilled.

INGREDIENTS

10 ounces oatmeal cookies

½ cup chopped or slivered almonds

½ cup (1 stick) plus 3 tablespoons butter, melted

10 ounces strawberries, sliced crosswise

18 ounces cream cheese

¾ cup plus 2 tablespoons sour cream

½ cup plus 5 teaspoons sugar

1 teaspoon vanilla extract

¾ cup plus 2 tablespoons heavy cream

Store-bought red cake glaze

Also required:
9-inch springform pan

BERLINER

 3 HOURS (INCL. RISING TIME)   20 PASTRIES  ★ ★ ★

These world-renowned pastries, usually filled with jam, have been known in Germany since the 16th century. The story goes that a pastry chef gave them a cannonball shape while serving as the baker for an army regiment. In Animal Crossing, Berliner pastries are only available on New Year's Eve. In real life, you can enjoy them anytime.

1. In a small bowl, combine the yeast, half of the milk (⅜ cup plus 1 tablespoon), and the salt. Allow the mixture to stand for 1 hour.

2. Meanwhile, in a large bowl, combine the butter, granulated sugar, and vanilla. Using an electric mixer, beat on medium speed until creamy, about 3 minutes. One at a time, add the egg and egg yolks, mixing thoroughly after each addition. Sift the flour into the bowl. Add the yeast mixture, vinegar, and remaining half of the milk and slowly and evenly combine until a smooth, soft dough forms.

3. Cover well with a clean kitchen towel and leave to rise in a warm place until the dough has doubled in size. How long this takes depends on various factors, but it will take at least 1 hour. Alternatively, preheat the oven to 125°F, then turn it off and set the covered bowl in the oven for about 30 minutes, or until the dough has doubled in size.

4. Transfer the dough to a floured surface and use your hands to pinch off 20 pieces of equal size. Roughly shape each one into a ball, making certain the tops are nice and smooth. Set the pieces of dough some distance apart on the counter and carefully cover with plastic wrap. Allow them to rise for 30 minutes. Then remove the plastic wrap and allow them to rise for another 30 minutes so a "skin" forms on the dough.

INGREDIENTS

1 cube fresh yeast

¾ cup plus 2 tablespoons whole milk

½ teaspoon salt

½ cup (1 stick) plus 1 tablespoon butter

2 tablespoons granulated sugar

1 tablespoon vanilla extract

1 egg

2 egg yolks

4 cups plus 2 tablespoons all-purpose flour, plus more for the counter

1 tablespoon vinegar

2 quarts (64 fluid ounces) high-quality neutral oil

5 ounces store-bought seedless raspberry jam

2 cups powdered sugar

Also required:
Pastry bag with medium-size tip

Kitchen thermometer

5. Meanwhile, heat the oil in a large, deep pot to 330° to 340°F. Working in batches, use a metal slotted spoon or skimmer to carefully slide the pastries, one at a time, into the hot oil with the tops facing down, until they are completely covered by the oil. Be sure not to overcrowd the pot. Cover the pot and deep-fry the pastries for 90 seconds, until golden brown. Then turn and cook on the other side for another 90 seconds. Turn again and cook the top for another 30 seconds. Use the slotted spoon to remove the cooked pastries and set them on a plate generously lined with paper towels to drain. Cover loosely with aluminum foil to keep warm. Repeat this process with the remaining dough.

6. Fill a pastry bag fitted with a medium tip with the raspberry jam. Carefully insert the tip into the middle of the pastry from the side and fill as desired with jam. Close the hole with a bit of pastry as needed so the jam does not drain out. Generously sprinkle the pastries with the powdered sugar. Best enjoyed promptly. Alternatively, store in a sealed airtight container lined with parchment paper.

BROWN SUGAR CUPCAKES

 40 MINUTES   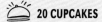 20 CUPCAKES   ★ ★

Cupcakes as such were first mentioned in 1796, in a cookbook titled *American Cookery*. They get their name from the fact that they used to be baked inside actual cups. But aside from the fact that specific cupcake pans are available these days, not much has changed about making cupcakes. This recipe is a staple for island residents, and will likely become one of your favorites, too. The cupcakes are a cinch to make, and just as tasty now as they were two hundred years ago.

1. Preheat the oven to 300°F. Set 20 cupcake liners on a baking sheet.

2. In a medium bowl, combine the yogurt, granulated and brown sugars, oil, and vanilla. Using an electric mixer set on medium speed, beat to combine well, 2 to 3 minutes. Add the eggs, one at a time, mixing after each addition. Add the flour and baking powder and mix until the batter is smooth and thick but still pourable. If it seems too stiff, add a bit of milk.

3. Use two tablespoons to divide the batter evenly among the liners. Bake for about 18 to 20 minutes, or until a toothpick inserted into the center of a cupcake comes out clean. Remove the pan from the oven and allow the cupcakes to cool completely.

4. Combine the powdered sugar and milk in a cup with a fork until no lumps remain. Add more powdered sugar or milk as needed. Brush the tops of the cooled cupcakes generously with glaze. Sprinkle with the chopped pistachios and allow the cupcakes to dry briefly.

5. Enjoy promptly or store in a sealed airtight container lined with parchment paper.

INGREDIENTS

¾ cup plus 2 tablespoons plain yogurt

1 cup granulated sugar

1 cup brown sugar

¾ cup plus 7 teaspoons neutral oil

1 tablespoon vanilla extract

3 eggs

3 cups all-purpose flour

1½ teaspoons baking powder

1 cup plus 2 tablespoons powdered sugar

3 to 4 tablespoons whole milk

2 ounces pistachios, coarsely chopped

Also required:
20 cupcake liners

DRINKS

Nothing says "island getaway" like relaxing with a cool, refreshing beverage. Or, if you're looking for a jolt of energy or to satisfy your sweet tooth, we've got that covered too. Like so much of Animal Crossing, the choice is yours.

COLORFUL JUICE

 5 MINUTES   2 SERVINGS   ⭐ ★

Life is especially vibrant in the world of Animal Crossing, where diversity and differences are celebrated. And what better way to toast such marvelous diversity than with this colorful, alcohol-free cocktail? In the game, you can get this special juice at Nook's Cranny. In the real world, you can simply make your own!

1. Use a ¾-inch melon baller to cut as many balls out of the apple as possible. Combine with the cocktail cherries and plums in a large pitcher.

2. Add the lemon juice, grapefruit juice, and liqueur. Fill with the soda and stir with a long spoon.

3. Transfer into tall glasses to serve. Add ice cubes (if using). Enjoy promptly.

INGREDIENTS

1 tart apple, peeled

10 cocktail cherries, drained

10 small jarred mirabelle plums, drained

3 tablespoons plus 1 teaspoon lemon juice

7 tablespoons grapefruit juice

¼ cup alcohol-free blue Curaçao liqueur

1 cup Sprite or other lemon-lime soda

Ice cubes (optional)

Also required:
¾-inch melon baller

MILKSHAKE

 5 MINUTES   1 SERVING   ★

Milkshakes have a long history, especially in the United States, where they are commonly found at fast-food restaurants, diners, and cafés. On your island, you can get a wide range of shakes at Nook's Cranny and the Paradise Planning office, among other places. But *this* delicious and refreshing vanilla-banana milkshake with whipped cream and caramel bits is only available in the real world . . . once you make it.

1. Put the banana pieces in a large mixing cup. Add the ice cream and milk and purée with an immersion blender until smooth.

2. Transfer to a tall serving glass, top with canned whipped topping, and sprinkle with a bit of caramelized nut crunch topping.

3. Enjoy right away.

INGREDIENTS

1 banana, coarsely chopped

2 scoops vanilla ice cream

¾ cup plus 2 tablespoons whole milk

Canned whipped topping

Hazelnut or almond crocant (store-bought caramelized nut crunch topping) for garnish

BOBA STRAWBERRY TEA

 40 MINUTES 2 SERVINGS   ★

Boba tea is hugely popular right now, in Animal Crossing as well as the real world. But it isn't easy to get this refreshing drink in AC, since you can only find it during the spectacular fireworks display at Harv's Island, and even then only if good fortune smiles on you. Enjoying a boba strawberry tea will refill your energy, but the tea disappears from your inventory after just three sips, and you have to re-enter the raffle if you want seconds. In real life, though, you can refill your cup as many times as you want—without having to win Redd's raffle first!

1. Prepare the tea according to the instructions on the package, making sure to brew it very strong. Allow it to cool briefly, then refrigerate.

2. Transfer the tapioca pearls to a small pot of water over high heat and bring to a boil. Cook until the pearls start to rise to the surface, about 3 to 5 minutes. Then lower the heat to medium and simmer for another 30 minutes, until the pearls take on a nice white color inside and have a gummy texture.

3. Transfer the cooked pearls to a strainer and rinse with cold water, then combine with the strawberry syrup in a medium bowl. Stir well to combine and let stand for 2 minutes so the flavors can meld. Then immediately divide evenly between two glasses.

4. Put the ice cubes in a cocktail shaker. Add the cold tea and milk and shake vigorously for 20 seconds. Pour evenly over the tapioca pearls (without the ice). Sweeten with more syrup as needed.

5. Enjoy promptly.

INGREDIENTS

6 bags black tea

5 ounces tapioca pearls

¼ cup strawberry syrup, plus more as needed

Handful ice cubes

¼ cup whole milk

Also required:
Cocktail shaker

MELON SODA

 5 MINUTES   1 SERVING   ★

Vacation is always the nicest part of the year, not just in the real world, but also for the residents of Animal Crossing. Anything that puts people in a vacation mood is really popular there, from Hawaiian shirts with a pineapple print to sunglasses and, of course, the right food and drinks. Melon soda is especially popular with the neighbors, which shouldn't come as too much of a surprise. After all, it doesn't get much better than sitting out on the veranda of your vacation home, enjoying the sun and the view of the ocean as you sip a refreshing cold glass of soda!

1. Place a large scoop of ice cream in the bottom of a highball glass.

2. Fill the glass with the melon soda up to about two finger widths from the brim. Stir in the lemon juice. Add the green food coloring and stir with a long spoon.

3. Generously top with whipped topping and garnish with the cherry. Serve immediately.

INGREDIENTS

1 large scoop vanilla ice cream

1 cup plus 2 tablespoons cold melon soda

1 tablespoon lemon juice

1 to 2 drops green food coloring

Canned whipped topping for garnish

1 fresh cherry or cocktail cherry

Also required:
Highball glass

CHERRY SMOOTHIE

 5 MINUTES   4 SERVINGS   ★

Cheri is a peppy bear cub who makes a wide variety of tasty fruit smoothies at her place, including this cherry one. The smoothie was supposedly invented in California in the 1970s, but that's not the whole story. In fact, markets in South and Central America have been selling *jugo,* or juice, for generations. Their version is a thick nectar made from fruit blended right then and there. Maybe you can use your new smoothie expertise to score some points with Claudia the next time you talk to her!

1. Combine the cherries, strawberries, and blueberries with the vanilla in a mixing cup and purée with an immersion blender.

2. Divide the fruit purée among four glasses, add 1 to 2 ice cubes to each one (if using), and fill each to the top with the sparkling water. Stir carefully with a long-handled spoon and enjoy promptly.

INGREDIENTS

9 ounces canned sweet cherries, drained

3.5 ounces frozen strawberries, thawed

2 ounces frozen blueberries, thawed

1 teaspoon vanilla extract

4 to 8 ice cubes (optional)

1¾ cups sparkling water

ICED CAFFÈ LATTE

CONTAINS ALCOHOL

 2 MINUTES 1 SERVING   ★

Coffee is generally very popular in Animal Crossing. And all the residents who drink it have very particular notions of how their favorite coffee should be brewed and served. Take Amelia, for example. She prefers Blue Mountain beans with lots of milk and three spoonfuls of sugar, while Rocco likes Mocha beans and only takes his black. But this drink, an irresistible mix of espresso, milk, caramel, and crushed ice, will wow any coffee lover, and even those who are lukewarm on coffee!

1. In a cocktail shaker, combine the advocaat, coffee, milk, sugar, and ice cubes and shake vigorously for 15 seconds.

2. Pour the coffee drink and ice cubes into a suitable glass. Garnish with whipped topping (if using) and serve promptly.

INGREDIENTS

4 teaspoons egg nog or advocaat

⅓ cup plus 2 tablespoons cold strong coffee

2 tablespoons plus 2 teaspoons whole milk

1 to 2 teaspoons sugar

Handful ice cubes

Canned whipped topping for garnish (optional)

Also required: Cocktail shaker

TIP OF THE DAY

To make this nonalcoholic, use store-bought egg nog without alcohol instead of advocaat. You can even add 1 teaspoon of vanilla extract to give this beverage an added kick of flavor.

ICED LEMON TEA

 45 MINUTES (INCL. COOLING TIME)   **5 SERVINGS**   ★

Is there anything more refreshing than a glass of ice-cold iced tea on a warm summer day? That's why we should all be grateful for Richard Blechynden, a Brit who introduced it at the St. Louis World's Fair in 1904. In Animal Crossing, enjoying this iced lemon tea lets you relocate trees and break rocks. In real life, you'll have to settle for quenching your thirst and beating the heat . . . not a bad deal!

1. Bring the water to a boil in a kettle. Place the teabags in a heat-resistant pitcher and pour in the hot water. Steep for 3 minutes, then remove the teabags.

2. Halve two of the lemons and juice them. Thinly slice the third lemon into rounds.

3. Add the lemon juice and slices to the tea, reserving five slices. Add the sugar and stir well until the sugar has fully dissolved. Refrigerate for 30 minutes.

4. To serve, divide the ice cubes among each of five highball glasses. Pour 1 tablespoon of strawberry syrup into each glass. Pour the lemon tea into the glasses and serve garnished with one lemon slice each.

INGREDIENTS

4 cups water

4 bags black tea

3 organic lemons

½ cup sugar

10 ice cubes

5 tablespoons strawberry syrup

Also required:
5 highball glasses

TAKEOUT COFFEE

 5 MINUTES   2 SERVINGS   ★

Coffee is said to be a mood lifter and energizer. We've known that since about 900 A.D., when an Ethiopian goatherd named Kaldi from the region of Kaffa noticed that his goats became very energetic after eating coffee beans off the bushes where they were growing. These days, coffee is available in many different varieties and styles of preparation. In the game, you can get this coffee to go from Brewster at The Roost. Lazy Stitches is a big fan, and once you've tried it, you'll know why!

1. Combine the instant coffee, sugar, and water in a measuring cup and stir well.

2. Beat with an electric mixer set on medium speed for about 3 minutes, or until the mixture forms a fluffy, thick coffee foam.

3. To serve, divide the plant-based milk and cold-brew coffee evenly between two cups and add ice cubes (if using). Pour the whipped coffee over the top, stir briefly, and enjoy!

INGREDIENTS

2 tablespoons instant coffee

2 tablespoons sugar

2 tablespoons boiling water

¾ cup plus 2 tablespoons
plant-based milk

¾ cup plus 2 tablespoons cold-brew
coffee of your choice

Ice cubes (optional)

COFFEE

DIETARY CONSIDERATIONS

STARTERS

	Dairy-Free	Gluten-Free	Vegan	Vegetarian
Salad-Stuffed Tomato		X		X
Olivier Salad	X	X		
Nanakusa Gayu		X		
Omurice		X		

SOUPS

	Dairy-Free	Gluten-Free	Vegan	Vegetarian
Bamboo-Shoot Soup	X			
Clam Chowder				
Minestrone Soup		X		
Pumpkin Soup				X
Seaweed Soup	X			

MAINS

	Dairy-Free	Gluten-Free	Vegan	Vegetarian
New Year's Noodles	X			
Gnocchi di Carote				X
Pad Krapow	X			
Curry with Rice		X		
Fish and Chips				
Pizza Margherita			X	X
Bread Gratin				X
Spaghetti Carbonara				X
Dungeness Crab Gratin				
Shoyu Ramen	X			
Veggie Quiche				X
Poke	X			
Pilaf		X		
Squid-Ink Spaghetti	X			

SIDES

	Dairy-Free	Gluten-Free	Vegan	Vegetarian
Baked Potatoes		X		X
Risotto		X		X
Potato Galette		X		X
Ketchup Fried Rice	X	X		X

SWEETS & DESSERTS

	Dairy-Free	Gluten-Free	Vegan	Vegetarian
Fruit Salad	X	X		X
Coconut Pancakes				X

(continued)

	Dairy-Free	Gluten-Free	Vegan	Vegetarian
Pompompurin Pudding				X
Pear Jelly	X	X		
Dango	X	X	X	X
Kerokerokeroppi Snack				X
Songpyeon	X	X		X

BAKED GOODS

	Dairy-Free	Gluten-Free	Vegan	Vegetarian
Frosted Pretzels				X
Pull-apart Bread				X
Chocolate Heart				X
Bûche de Noël				X
Apple Pie				X
Cake Salé				X
Carrot Cake				X
Thumbprint Jam Cookies				X
Fruit Scones				X
Orange Pie				X
Birthday Cake				X
Snack Bread				X
Moon Cakes	X			X
Surichwi Tteok	X		X	X
Spooky Cookies				X
Mom's Homemade Cake				X
Berliner				X
Brown Sugar Cupcakes				X

DRINKS

	Dairy-Free	Gluten-Free	Vegan	Vegetarian
Colorful Juice	X	X	X	X
Milkshake		X		X
Boba Strawberry Tea		X		X
Melon Soda		X		X
Cherry Smoothie	X	X	X	X
Iced Caffè Latte		X		X
Iced Lemon Tea	X	X	X	X
Takeout Coffee	X	X	X	X

CONVERSION CHARTS

VOLUME

U.S.	METRIC
$^1/_5$ teaspoon	1 ml
1 teaspoon	5 ml
1 tablespoon	15 ml
1 fluid ounce	30 ml
$^1/_5$ cup	50 ml
$^1/_4$ cup	60 ml
$^1/_3$ cup	80 ml
$^1/_2$ cup	120 ml
$^2/_3$ cup	160 ml
$^3/_4$ cup	180 ml
1 cup	240 ml
1 pint (2 cups)	480 ml
1 quart (4 cups)	1 l

TEMPERATURES

FAHRENHEIT	CELSIUS
200°	93.3°
212°	100°
250°	120°
275°	135°
300°	150°
325°	165°
350°	177°
400°	205°
425°	220°
450°	233°
475°	245°
500°	260°

WEIGHT

U.S.	METRIC
0.5 ounces	14 grams
1 ounces	28 grams
$^1/_4$ pound	113 grams
$^1/_3$ pound	151 grams
$^1/_2$ pound	227 grams
1 pound	454 grams

PO Box 15
Cobb, CA 95426

ISBN: 978-1-958862-02-5

Created by Grinning Cat Productions
Written by Tom Grimm
Photography by: Tom Grimm and Dimitrie Harder
Typesetting, Cover, and Layout: Dennis Winkler
Special thanks to Roberts Urlovskis!

Manufactured in China

10 9 8 7 6 5 4 3 2 1